THE HISTORY OF
WESSEX COACHES LTD

A COMPANY WITH TWO FACES

THE HISTORY OF WESSEX COACHES LTD

A Company with two faces

By John Sealey

AMBERLEY

First published 2009

Amberley Publishing Plc
Cirencester Road, Chalford,
Stroud, Gloucestershire, GL6 8PE

www.amberley-books.com

British Library Cataloguing in Publication Data.
A catalogue record for this book is available from the British Library.

ISBN 978 1 84868 243 6

Typesetting and Origination by diagrafmedia
Printed in Great Britain

Contents

Acknowledgements

I owe sincere thanks to a number of people who have allowed me to broaden my memories and knowledge in the preparation of this work.

Firstly, my thanks to Raymond Jones, an ex-Director of Wessex Coaches Ltd. my ex-boss and a friend of many years. He and I have spent many happy hours reminiscing, which enabled me to compile a great deal of this work. To Mr G.T. Jones, who has not been too well of late and, whilst not being able to add any practical help, was able to show his full appreciation and endorsement when shown a proof copy of the work. I wish him well.

To Derek Jones, the son of G.T. Jones, who discovered some previously unseen family photos from the archives. To Mrs Pat Dorgan, daughter of Walter Feltham, for allowing me full access to her late father's autobiography. To Henry Everett, an ex-employee of both Maple Leaf and Wessex and a very long-standing friend. Henry was involved in the two complete vehicle rebuilds in Wessex workshops in 1948.

My thanks to Geoff Lusher for providing the history of his late father's position within the company and for his help in editing the work, together with the provision of family and company photos. To John Mosedale and Roger Grimley for their help with the Chard & District history. To David Cheesley, himself a local historian and author.

To all of the anonymous photographers whose pictures, not only from my own collection but that of Geoff Bruce and the Colin Gittins collection, have been used in this book. Whilst all attempts have been made to contact the original copyright holders of identifiable pictures used, this has not always been possible and for this I can only apologise. Acknowledgements have been made, where appropriate, throughout the book. The pictures of ex-Leicester vehicles are attributed to Mr Brian Coney and Mr Peter Newland, whilst the ex-Leeds pictures, together with many others, are from my own collections gathered over many years from many rally visits, etc.

Finally, to my wife for allowing me to spend many, many hours over a period of three years, either sat in front of a computer or being dragged to various places and rallies to seek out more factual material for this work.

My sincere thanks to everyone involved.

Introduction

My father was a tram conductor, and later a bus driver with Bristol Tramways (BT&CC Ltd) for many years. My maternal grandfather had worked for Greyhound Motors as a conductor. So I suppose that an interest in transport began at birth.

I joined Wessex Coaches Ltd (hereafter 'Wessex') and enjoyed my time with the company, but after six years I decided to move to pastures new and left the passenger-vehicle field. My memories stayed with me, and I continued in part-time employment up to 1983. I remained in touch with the industry, but was employed in selling to the transport and engineering industries up to the time of my retirement in the year 2000. I was a long-term associate member of the Institute of Road Transport Engineers (AMIRTE, AMSOE) until the year 2004.

In a moment of "retirement boredom" I decided that someone should sit down and write a history of what was, reputedly, one of the largest privately owned bus and coach companies in the UK. Wessex was also, so we believe, the largest operator in the UK of a fully Bedford/Duple fleet of front line vehicles. Apart from three Daimler CVD6 coaches, delivered in 1948, no other type of vehicle/body combination was ever purchased new by the company. In the compilation of this work I have received invaluable assistance from members of the Jones family with whom I have kept in touch over the years. I have been loaned copies of photographs and records from the family archives that have not been seen previously outside of the family. This has also been the case with the Kingswood Queen (Feltham's) fleet, so fortunately written by Walter Feltham in his lifetime and provided by his daughter, Mrs Pat Dorgan.

In the case of each of the fleets purchased since 1948, I have had to seek help from various sources outside of the family, but mainly from former employees; some I have kept in touch with over the years whilst others are new or renewed acquaintances.

I came late into the company, so can only draw upon my personal experiences of a limited period when the company had already been trading for about fourteen years. As I delved into the facts and sought out official records, I realised that my own experiences extended well beyond Wessex itself, and it is for that reason that many other companies, some of which I came into contact with in the course of my employment, merit a mention also.

All Bristolians recognized the red and grey-green, smartly turned out vehicles of "the Wessex" but, alas, the large fleet that was built up over a period of twenty-six years, plus the very many years of its forbears, came to an end when the business was sold to the National Bus Company on 1 August 1974.

Each of the major operators at the formation, together with three of the companies involved in takeovers through the years, have very interesting historical backgrounds. But I then discovered that some of those companies had themselves absorbed other fleets, and these required further investigation, which I will attempt to relate here together with my memories of the Bristol coaching scene in the 1960s.

I am sure that some people will maybe disagree with my version of events as I remember them and I would be only to pleased to hear from these people, if only to put my records straight and so provide an accurate history of this prestigious company for the sake of generations to come. I may be contacted through the publishers.

John Sealey, 2009

CHAPTER 1

Events leading to the formation of Wessex Coaches Ltd

Immediately after the Second World War, Morning Star Motor Services Ltd of Lawrence Hill and L.W. Andrews Ltd t/a Clifton Greys (of Clifton) were two of the largest motor coach companies in Bristol. In 1947 Mr George Jubilee Jones, Managing Director of Morning Star, formed an alliance with Mr Langdon William Andrews, Managing Director of Clifton Greys, to take over the vehicles, interests, services, property and goodwill of other Bristol-based operators. These included the road service licences of Maid of the Mountains Motor Coach Co. Ltd (C.W. Jordan); The Maple Leaf Garage (C.W. Jordan); Morning Star Motor Services Ltd; Forerunner Coaches of Redfield, Bristol; and L.W. Andrews Ltd t/a Clifton Greys. Wessex Coaches Ltd was registered in August 1947, but did not commence trading as a single entity until 15 April 1948, by which time all legal matters had been finalized. New licences had been applied for in the previous February.

In terms of vehicle numbers involved, Morning Star was the largest constituent of the amalgamation, with thirty vehicles. Clifton Greys contributed twenty-two vehicles, nineteen came from Maple Leaf Garages (C.W. Jordan Ltd), with a further five contributed by their associated fleet, C.W. Jordan t/a Maid of the Mountains Motor Coach Co. Ltd. In late 1946 Mr G.J. Jones had acquired an interest in the Forerunner Motor Coach Co. of Mr W.J. Williams & Sons (Redfield Coaches) of 275 Church Road, Redfield, Bristol. This fleet remained a subsidiary company until the formation of Wessex. Also included were the former Head Office building of Clifton Greys at 71/73, Whiteladies Road, and the garage and workshops formerly occupied by Maple Leaf at Clifton Road. A booking office at Colston Avenue also came from Maple Leaf, as did premises on Weston-Super-Mare seafront. A booking office at 17 Lawrence Hill from Morning Star survived into Wessex ownership, as did a building in Wellington Street (off Lawrence Hill), which was used up to the late 1960s as a vehicle paint shop. The new company was to be known as Wessex Coaches Ltd and had acquired seventy-six vehicles, making them the largest tours and excursions operator in Bristol, and what was claimed to be the largest all-coach fleet in the country.

At the formation, the Directors of Wessex Coaches Ltd were as follows: Mr L.W. Andrews, Mr E. Andrews Mr Bert. Andrews (all from Clifton Greys), Mr G.J. Jones, Mr W. Jones, Mr G.T. Jones, Mr R.L. Jones (from Morning Star). Mr Sydenham, a very prominent City of London accountant, became the Company Chairman. He was also Chairman of Duple Motor Bodies Ltd and other companies. As far as the shareholdings were concerned, these were split more or less equally between the two families and both had equal voting rights.

I take the following from a trade article published in 1953, which explains how the rolling stock and operational problems were initially visualised and overcome:

'Various makes of vehicle were operated by each of the companies involved in the amalgamation and Wessex took them over for the continuation of operation of the business. Excursions and Tours and Private Hire then constituted the entire business and this was a major factor in guiding the Directors to adopt certain principles. The senior directors were previously the principals of the constituent companies and had been primarily responsible for the makeup of the fleets taken over. They had previously had little or no choice of heavy or light vehicles in the 33-35 seat categories but, in 1948, the Bedford 29 seater Vista was available and, though perhaps smaller than ideal, became the preferred option. As independents they had each been happy with Duple bodies and, in consequence, Bedford chassis with Duple bodywork seemed to fit nicely into the plan. There was no great dissatisfaction with the heavyweight vehicles in the fleet, indeed, some of them had been on the road for many years and were good for many more. It was perhaps their capacity to give service during a prolonged life that put them at somewhat of a disadvantage in this undertaking. Their initial cost was in keeping with their long life but with a smaller annual mileage than had they been employed on express or even stage carriage workings, they suffered from one major complaint – obsolescence. When Wessex was formed it was agreed to give a book life of twenty years for all makes and models. Due allowance was made for the number of years already passed and book values were set to take into account the rising costs of replacement. And so it was decided that, for a coach with, say twelve years previous life, eight twentieths depreciation remained to be debited – plus a special depreciation allowance which had to go some of the way to covering the difference between the original purchase price in, say, 1935, and the replacement price in 1955. Only after these charges and the addition of all other operating expenses could any surplus be looked upon as profit. This special depreciation charge was a huge drain on profit. With the appearance in 1951 of the 37 seat Bedford Vega the directors foresaw a lessening of their problems. The full replacement values of the earlier "heavies" were no longer needed as a Vega could be purchased for well under £3000. This figure was such that a rethink was necessary and it was decided to depreciate each vehicle to fourteen years and so considerably reduce the obsolescence factor. As it turned out, running costs for the 29 and 37 seater

Bedfords, although low for petrol-engined vehicles, were higher than anticipated – further accentuated with a rise in fuel duty with the 1952 budget. To help meet this situation some of the Vistas were fitted with Perkins P6 diesel engines. A diesel-engined version of the Vega was, in 1953, eagerly awaited and by which time it was hoped to have eliminated the old stock. The fleet had by now been reduced to 67 and the directors felt that their operations were as economical as they would ever be as far as the vehicles were concerned. Below is a table which shows comparative M.P.G. figures for one month's operation of 47 petrol and diesel-engined vehicles. In the right hand column this has been calculated to a cost per seat mile, (in old pence) – obviously the main interest of the accountants of the day. The company hoped that, when the diesel engined variant of the Vega became available, the m.p.g. figure would improve and the cost per seat mile would be about .08d. Other costs must of course be kept to a minimum. Conflicting claims in an all-coach operation do not make this easy. On the one hand, it is desirable to keep well-trained and reliable drivers employed throughout the year. New, seasonal drivers are an unknown quantity; on the other hand any organisation can suffer if it retains too large a non-earning staff. Like other concerns Wessex compromised. Of the total of 67 vehicles operated in 1952, 37 were licensed for the whole year and drivers can, accordingly be kept but even these drivers are not fully employed in driving during the off-season and they join others whose services are retained wholly for vehicle overhaul purposes. The net result is that during the season proper it is necessary to recruit only about twelve drivers – a remarkably small number in relation to the size of the fleet. Several of these twelve come back year after year. Then, and for the lifetime of the company, Wessex undertook virtually all of its vehicle and body repairs and maintenance. Reference to drivers is perhaps a little misleading, for many of the men are engaged primarily as fitters, bodybuilders or painters and then, if not already qualified, are trained to drive. The men in the shops were, with few exceptions, badge holding craftsmen. For a time after the amalgamation, when the whole fleet consisted of heavier units, the body-shop rebodied some chassis but this is no longer considered economic (in 1952) as the remaining heavies are on their way out and the Bedfords are, as previously mentioned, destined for a 14 year life and not likely to need new bodies during that time. Half the fleet was repainted in alternate years therefore more than 30 coaches went through the paint-shop each year. On the traffic side it became quite clear that Wessex was benefitting as a single entity rather than the five operating units as previous. This was attributed to the fact that Bristol, like most other cities of comparable size, contains artisan, medium and residential districts. The effect was to spread the demand. A predominantly working-class district, for example, contains a large number of people whose annual holiday was taken around early August whilst in a residential area many people avoided that time whenever possible. At the time of formation the Wessex season extended from Whit Saturday to the end of October. By 1952/3 that had curiously contracted to finish at the end of September and the directors attributed this largely to succeeding Chancellors of the Exchequer whose budgets have affected the mainstay of the Wessex business – the landlords and pensioned classes who normally decide on late holidays. Fostering travel was of course one of the prime functions of Wessex and its staff. Guided by experience the company included some 80% of its private hire business in the "comprehensive" category whereby the charge includes meals, etc. as well as actual travel. Eight day tours were arranged from Sunday to Sunday for the benefit of people with one clear week's holiday and popular tours were scheduled to fall on different days of the week so that shopkeepers governed by early closing days could get their turn with others restricted in different ways.'

Fortunately, fuel prices were reduced in late 1952, so maybe the forecast figures mentioned were further improved upon. Bear in mind also that these figures are in old currency units, and 12*d* became 5 modern pence at decimalisation.

	No. of vehicles	Seating Capacity	Fuel	Miles per gallon	Cost per mile	Cost per seat
Daimler	10	33	Diesel	12.96	3.396*d*	0.10*d*
Leyland	2	35	Petrol	7.85	5.859*d*	0.17*d*
Leyland	2	35	Diesel	13.85	3.176*d*	0.09*d*
Leyland	6	33	Diesel	12.98	3.389*d*	0.10*d*
Bedford Vista	8	29	Diesel	17.27	2.547*d*	0.07*d*
Bedford Vista	13	29	Petrol	11.39	4.038*d*	0.14*d*
Bedford Vega	6	37	Petrol	9.53	4.827*d*	0.13*d*

On those figures, incidentally, one gallon of diesel fuel cost 1*s* 6½*d* (.077p), whilst petrol cost just over 1*s* 7*d* (.0798) per gallon.

This is a rare picture from the family album, taken six years after the formation of the company, and on the occasion of the delivery of the twelve new 38-seat Bedford Vegas coaches in 1954. *Left to Right:* Bert Andrews, Bill Jones, Alec Lusher, Ernie Andrews, L.W. Andrews, G.J. Jones, G.T. ('young George') Jones, Harry Lewis, Frank Davis and Raymond Jones.

CHAPTER 2

Morning Star

Mr Edward Caleb (Ted) Jones had commenced charabanc operation in 1919, having already operated horses and lorries on general haulage work for some years. The earliest passenger-carrying vehicle recorded was probably a 'brake' body placed onto a Leyland lorry chassis and registered AE6543. The bodies would have been inter-changeable. The registration dates the event as 1916. By the early 1920s Ted had established some local excursions business, private hire and a taxi service, and other vehicles were obtained in 1921-22. In March 1923 E. Jones and Sons Ltd, t/a Morning Star Coach Services Ltd, was formed and a number of "heavyweight" vehicles came into the scene in 1922-24. These were probably for use on the London services, as mentioned later. Ted Jones had four sons, George, William, Charlie and Jim (there were two daughters also), all actively engaged in the business at some time or another. Ted expected his pound of flesh from everyone, be he or she family-member or employee. It can be said that each of the boys fell out with their father at some time or another and went off to do other things. But George and Bill seem to be the two that, having left and come back a few times, stuck with the business. Charlie appears to have had little involvement in the family firm. Jim joined the Merchant Navy prior to the war and served as an engineer on Elders & Fyffes boats, but came back to the business upon the death of his father in 1942. He continued to work as a driver for the duration, but went on to become a very successful business man in his own right with a large engineering business after the war. Ted Jones was a hard man who had won civil awards for his bravery – more about him later. Stories have been told of the old chap sacking a man and chasing him off the premises with a high-pressure hose ... and then re-employing him the next day when he was short of a driver.

It is a known fact that Bristol Greyhound ran the world's first daily passenger motor vehicle service between two major cities – Bristol & London. Many

Another from the Jones' family album. Ted and Mrs Jones are stood on the steps, with Mrs Jones holding Jim in her arms. The child held by Ted Jones died as an infant. The two daughters are stood on the cart. The rest I am guessing – I imagine that Charlie is the young lad on the cart. The man holding the horse in the centre appears to be a little older than the other two, so I guess that the horses on the left and right are held by George and Bill respectively.

TE 4468 was a Leyland SWQ2 ten-tonner, built in 1928 and supplied new to E. Jones and Sons Ltd as fleet no. 18 and chassis no. 16676. By my reckoning it is carrying a load consisting of eighty-seven 45-gallon oil drums and, assuming that these were full, would be carrying an almost capacity load. Note the dual headlights (oil and electric) and also the solid tyres which I would have thought to have been a rather dated feature in 1928. I am indebted to Mike Sutcliffe for this concise and detailed chassis information.

The premises of Morning Star Motors Ltd. The picture is taken some time after 1933, when this trading title was first used. G.H. Hill was a potato merchant with premises next door, and it appears that this photo is posed on their behalf, as Morning Star occupied the premises on the right up to the time of the amalgamation in 1947.

local operators were envious of this service and wanted a slice of the cake for themselves – Morning Star was one of these. They had their programme of day tours of course, from Lawrence Hill, but in March 1928 Morning Star Services decided to enter the long-distance field with the inauguration of their own daily service to London. Apparently, there was friendly rivalry with several companies by now operating the service, and a fare standardization was agreed whereby the passenger paid 10s 6d per single journey and 20s (£1) return. As always happens, along came an out-of-town operator who was prepared to cut these prices to 9s (45p) single and 15s (75p) return; Morning Star decided to follow suit. The initial service operated to London via Bath, Marlborough and Reading, but it was soon decided that there were signs of passenger traffic (both direct and part-stage) on alternative routes: through Faringdon, Oxford and High Wycombe, for example. Two more coaches were acquired and a second London service began covering this route. It is recorded that loadings were heavier than anticipated on this route, particularly through the winter months of 1928/9. From early July 1928 until the following January a daily service was run from Bristol to Torquay, but this did not prove so successful and was suspended for the remainder of the winter months to resume again in April 1929. Greyhound carried conductors on their services, and the Bristol Watch Committee decided that a second man was indeed required by all operators while within the city boundaries. At the first application for licence renewals, it was ruled that a conductor be carried at all times, as the journeys were treated as long-distance bus services with intermediate stops in all towns and villages through which they passed. At this time the Watch Committee also decided (in the case of Morning

Star at least) that the inward and outbound routes were to be changed so that each travelled over different roads. Morning Star appealed to this restriction, as firstly, this added one extra mile per journey and secondly, it was suggested that the route inbound was through the poorer districts and would give the visitor a bad impression of the city.

Morning Star laid great stress upon the maintenance of the route timetables, and the success achieved was largely attributed to the good work of the drivers in this connection. One year on only one scheduled journey had failed to materialize, and this was apparently 'due to circumstances beyond the company's control' and was quite unavoidable – no passengers were ever left stranded. The percentage of late-running was maintained at 'an exceedingly low level'. In the trade press of April 1929 this admirable record was accredited to the business methods of the company, to the drivers, and, of course, to the vehicles, which by now were all Leyland Lion/Lioness chassis with bodies by either United Automobile Services or Davies & Son of Horfield, Bristol. At the end of the first year of these operations, more vehicles were on order to the same specification. Adverts of the time pointed out that the Lionesses had the same type of chassis and engine as to those supplied to HM King George V, with 29.9hp (59bhp) engines that provided 'remarkable' acceleration and ample power for the hills like Tog Hill (when the journey was sometimes varied), Derry Hill (Calne), and Marlborough Hill on the London route. The vehicles were each plated in Bristol. Each of the bodies on the Leylands was to a luxury specification with individual armchair seating, and they were billed as "Super Comfort Coaches". I am certain that they gave a much more comfortable ride than the Bristol B & D types then (1928) operated by Bristol Greyhound.

HW 658 was a 1928 Leyland Lion (PLC1) with a United 26-seat body used by Morning Star on the express services. It is seen here at the London terminus in Spring Street, Paddington, W2, and looks ready to set off on the long return journey to Bristol. This vehicle passed to Greyhound Motors in 1933 and later became a service bus in Bristol.

A newspapaer advert of the time.

1930 SMC (Sunbeam) Pathan. C26D short body, purchased for the express services; it lasted well until 1942.

An unidentified picture of a Morning Star vehicle and party, but we do know that G.J. Jones is the driver.

Above: 1925 Dennis four-tonner. One of the first-generation long-distance vehicles.

Left: A Bristol Greyhound advertisment.

HU 4805 was a 1926 AEC, Model No. 411, and one of the vehicles with which Greyhound Motors Ltd later operated their daily Bristol to London service. Note the pneumatic tyres. The location appears to be Hammersmith Broadway, with the bus about to enter King Street for the return. This was the route used by all vehicles prior to the 1961 opening of the Cromwell Road extension and Chiswick Flyover as we know it today.

Greyhound Motors Ltd of Bristol commenced their daily operation of the London service in February 1925. Dennises with solid tyres were used initially, and, as the photos show, AEC vehicles soon followed, with pneumatic tyres. Solid-tyred vehicles would have had a 12mph speed restriction but with pneumatics this was raised to 20mph. The AECs were advertised as 'Luxurious Travelling Parlours', taking a full 8 hours to complete the journey via Bath, Marlborough, Newbury, Reading and Maidenhead (the route of the old A4 and terminating at Hammersmith Broadway), but appear later to have dropped off at certain West End hotels. Two coaches a day were operated by Greyhound, leaving Colston Street at 9am and 11am. The 9am departure travelled direct via Chippenham and arrived in London at 5pm, but the 11am departure diverted from the A4 at Box to proceed via Melksham and Devizes to rejoin the A4 at Beckhampton. The records state that these coaches ran on solid tyres and this is confirmed by the photo of HU 1176, a Dennis 4-tonner; but operators were certainly fitting pneumatics as standard by 1925, and the other photo shows HU 4805, a pneumatic-tyred AEC vehicle, new in March 1926 bearing out this statement. Bristol B & D types were later used from 1927 onward and these had then become 'Super De Luxe Buffet

Coaches'. Each sumptuous, individual red antique leather seat had a folding table, the windows were curtained and there was a steward's pantry for tea, cigarettes and chocolate. Each coach had smoking and non-smoking sections.

By January 1933 Morning Star had succumbed to the Greyhound opposition, having encountered severe financial difficulties. It would appear that Bristol Greyhound, now with the might of Bristol Tramways behind them, had far more resources available to them than any competitor. Thus the services were sold, together with the four Lions and four Lionesses to Greyhound Motors in 1933 leaving them with little or no further opposition on the London run. Greyhound Motors had been controlled by Bristol Tramways and Carriage Co. Ltd since 1928, but it was not until 1936 that the company was wound up and passed into the full ownership of Bristol Tramways. An interesting fact here: among the seventy-five vehicles transferred in 1936 to BT&CC were the eight Morning Star vehicles. Four were retained as coaches for a short time, but the other four had already been demoted to bus work by Greyhound. All eight had been scrapped by the early '40s. Greyhound Motors operated from their registered office at 96, West Street, Old Market, and from a garage around the corner in Trinity Street, St Philips, which still stands today, albeit latterly as a tyre supplier's workshop and now standing empty and To Let. Its future is uncertain. This garage was retained by BT&CC until the early '50s, and I remember coaches being parked there for the duration of the war. The doors were always kept closed, as I remember, but, as a small lad, I used to peep through the cracks in the doors at the vehicles inside. To this day I remember seeing in there the Duple-bodied Bristol L5Gs that were delivered immediately prior to the outbreak of the war, and, if not commandeered at some time, would have been virtually brand new when put back on the road in 1946/7. I always thought that these were quite handsome vehicles.

With the cash-injection that the sale of vehicles and services gave them, Morning Star was financially restructured in 1933 and registered as Morning Star Motor Services Ltd. E. Jones & Sons Ltd still operated motor lorries on general haulage work and, indeed, did so until after the Second World War ended. Several old charabanc chassis are known to have passed to 'E. Jones, Bristol', for further use as lorries. Morning Star Motor Services Ltd carried on, expanded the tours and excursions as well as their private hire business, and continued to sometimes run 'on hire' to Greyhound Motors for the London services.

Older ex-Morning Star drivers told me, at the time of my employment, that it was usual practice to come in on a Friday night during the 1930s, after a day's lorry driving, and take the body off the lorry, put a brake body on the chassis and immediately duplicate a London service to return on Saturday. I remember Les Jay telling me that on a Saturday night, the last service left Marlborough at 10.30pm. No standing passengers were legally permitted on the coaches, but the coach always left Marlborough with about twenty-five unseated. The driver would have been lynched had he refused these passengers, who had probably been sampling the wares of the town's hostelries all day. Out of the town the law would be waiting, but could only sympathize with the driver and send him on his way.

Morning Star's garage was situated at 55, Lawrence Hill, and remained so until 1947. This property backed onto 30 Easton Road, which was a one-time private address of the Jones family, and this address does appear on some publications. Premises at 17 Lawrence Hill were used as a booking office. Around the corner in Wellington Street was a shed which was probably originally used for maintenance, but in the time of Wessex was utilized as the paint shop. Each of those premises is now buried forever beneath the approaches to the Lawrence Hill roundabout of the inner ring road. There is also evidence that property at 13 Clarence Road, Bedminster, was used. I recall these large garage premises being occupied commercially in about 1950 by a company called Victoria Garage, and later by Osmond's of Curry Rivel, who used it as a Bristol base for their coaches. Morning Star's livery was predominantly red with cream relief and gold lettering. A gold star motif was used on the lower side panels. Leyland dominated both new and second-hand purchases.

Morning Star Leyland charabanc FR 4349 in 1927-8. It is seen here with a load of happy ladies – I wonder how many hats blew away on that day trip. Note the pneumatic tyres. This one carried fleet no. 9, but by the end of 1930 had donated its chassis to a lorry in the haulage fleet. G.J. Jones is the driver and Raymond has identified his mother as the lady sat to George's right.

Ted Jones in the front passenger seat. The car is a 1931 Crossley 24hp

XJ 6772 Leyland Tiger TS4 was originally owned by a Manchester operator before passing to Baxter of Airdrie. Morning Star purchased it in 1943 and it received a new Duple body in 1946. It lasted until 1958 and was probably in a batch of vehicles part-exchanged to Arlington Motors for the DHY series of Bedford Super Vegas.

CK 4339 was one of three Leyland Tigers purchased in 1939 from Ribble of Preston. Originally 30-seater buses, they were re-bodied by Duple in 1939 with C32F bodies. Requisitioned by the Royal Navy in June 1943 they were returned (via a dealer) in July 1944. Each of the three lasted until 1954.

KHU 47 Bedford OB. New to Morning Star in 1947, it passed to Wessex lasting until late 1957.

George Jones (Snr) about to board at Lawrence Hill (*c.* 1947) with a bunch of friends embarking upon a 'men only' outing. George (Jnr) is the young man in the front of picture. Tom Cox is the driver.

A very interesting picture from 1947 during the last season of operation by Morning Star. The picture shows four Leyland Tigers and a newly acquired Bedford WTL, which appear to be about to depart Lawrence Hill on a tour. The drivers and staff can be identified from left to right as Mr G.J.Jones, Ted Cox, [unknown], Alec Lusher, George Prew, Tom Cox and [unknown]. There are several interesting features of this picture. TF 6616 was sold by Morning Star to a dealer later that season, but it was purchased by Wessex in 1949, albeit with a new body by Lee Motors of Bournemouth. George Prew transferred to Wessex and worked for them for the life of the company, finishing as a no.1 extended-tour driver. It must have taken at least ten minutes to arrange and park these vehicles which are shown to be blocking off half of what was a very busy thoroughfare, which leads me to think that it was taken on a Sunday afternoon. Apart from TF 6616, the other three Leylands and the newly purchased Bedford all went into the Wessex fleet. The picture of TF 6616 in its rebuilt state is shown elsewhere.

Certificate No. 273548.

THE COMPANIES ACTS, 1929 AND 1947.

COMPANY LIMITED BY SHARES.

SPECIAL AND EXTRAORDINARY RESOLUTIONS
— OF —
MORNING STAR MOTORS LIMITED.

Passed 15th day of April, 1948.

At an EXTRAORDINARY GENERAL MEETING of the above-named Company held at Queens Road Garage, Clifton, in the City and County of Bristol, on Thursday the 15th day of April, 1948, the following RESOLUTIONS were passed as SPECIAL and EXTRAORDINARY RESOLUTIONS respectively :—

SPECIAL RESOLUTIONS.

1. That the Company be wound up voluntarily and that Mr. Arnold George Warham Scott of 27, Martin Lane, London, E.C.4, be and is hereby appointed Liquidator for the purpose of such winding up.

2. That the said Liquidator is hereby empowered and authorised :—

(a) To execute and do all such assurances acts and things as may be necessary and required by law for the purpose of transferring to and vesting in Wessex Coaches Limited (hereinafter called "Wessex") the whole of the business assets and undertaking of the Company (except as expressly excepted thereby) for the purpose of carrying into effect the terms and provisions of an Agreement under Seal dated the 7th day of January, 1948, made between the Company of the one part and Wessex of the other part as amended and varied by a Supplemental Agreement under Seal and between the same parties dated the 19th day of March, 1948, being agreements for the sale by the Company to Wessex (except as therein mentioned) of all the undertaking assets and business of the Company as therein more particularly specified.

(b) To receive as consideration or compensation for the said sale fully paid Preference and Ordinary Shares in the capital of Wessex (of the number and value in the Agreements provided) for distribution among the contributories of the Company and in particular and without prejudice to the generality of the foregoing to direct on behalf of the Company that the whole or any part of the said consideration by way of fully paid up Preference and Ordinary Shares in the capital of Wessex Coaches Limited (as the Liquidator may think fit) be allotted and issued to the contributories of the Company.

EXTRAORDINARY RESOLUTIONS.

3. Pursuant to Article 25 of the Articles of Association of the Company in so far as the same shall not be required for the purpose of the liquidation and the payment of the debts liabilities and obligations of the Company whether ascertained contingent or future the Liquidator is hereby authorised to allocate distribute and divide in specie amongst the contributories shareholders and Members of the Company (according to their respective rights and in such manner as the said Liquidator shall think fit) all the surplus assets of the Company of any nature whatsoever.

4. That the said Liquidator is hereby authorised and entitled to exercise any of the powers given by Paragraphs (d). (e) and (f) of Sub-section 1 of Section 191 of the Companies Act, 1929, to a Liquidator in a winding up by the Court.

G. J. JONES,
Chairman.

As shown, Morning Star was formally wound up in April 1948 when all assets passed to Wessex Coaches Ltd.

At the formation of Wessex in 1948, Mr G.J. Jones together with his sons, G.T. Jones and R.L. Jones became directors of Wessex, as did Mr W. (Bill) Jones, (brother of G.J.). Mr G.J. Jones passed away in 1970, and Bill died in 1969, three months after his retirement. George and Raymond are still about, although George has not enjoyed the best of health for the past few years. Interestingly, at the time of his appointment Raymond was carrying out his National Service in Egypt, and he still has the copy of the letter confirming his directorship.

In 1947 the road haulage business of E. Jones and Sons Ltd was disposed of to Pioneer Transport Ltd, Bristol, and in turn, Pioneer's business was nationalized upon the formation of Road Haulage Executive.

CHAPTER 3

Clifton Greys

L.W. Andrews was probably the oldest-established of the original pre-Wessex operators as a passenger carrying concern. We know that a livery stable business was established by 1905 at Abbotsford Mews, Redland, Bristol, and was successful to the extent that, by 1915, two further stables were operating, one at Tyndalls Park Road, Clifton, and the other at Cornwallis Mews, Clifton. By 1915 the repair, maintenance and hire of motor cars was also being undertaken, and the company was able to offer a transport service almost as comprehensive as that offered by the mighty Bristol Tramways & Carriage Co., and most certainly rivalled them in the Clifton and Redland districts of the city.

Charabancs came along in 1919 and were operated under the name of 'Clifton Greys', a reference to the equestrian 'fleet'. An office was opened at 73 Whiteladies Road in 1919 to deal with the new charabanc venture. L.W. Andrews Limited (t/a Clifton Greys) was registered in 1930 and formally wound up in April 1948, when all assets again passed to Wessex Coaches Ltd. By the early '30s 'The Greys' operated more than twenty vehicles; the business was thriving, but the horse and motorcar side of the business was on the decline and the 'charas' therefore became the main interest of the company.

Daimler, Napier, Lancia AEC & Reo types were used in the early days and, in 1931, six locally built BAT chassis entered the fleet. From the mid-'20s second-hand acquisitions also featured, mostly Reos, ADC and Daimlers. L.W. Andrews passed away around 1954, and his sons Ernie and Bert were left as the only active members of the family working in the business, although other family members retained their shares. Ernie unfortunately died while on his way to visit Duples in 1962, and it was at this time that Bert retired. It is interesting to note that 73 Whiteladies Road, together with the adjoining property, No. 71, became the registered office of Wessex Coaches upon formation, and survived as such until the very end. Indeed, this must have been a very lucrative move to have kept

1907 Humber Taxicab at Abbotsford Mews garage.

An early Clifton Greys vehicle. This is a 1921 14-seat Napier, either HT 3223 or HT 3224.

An unidentified picture of a load of happy young ladies in a 14-seat Napier,

HU 27 was a 20-seat Napier, owned by Clifton Greys from 1924 to 1932.

DF 5185 was a 1928 Reo GB with a C20F body by London Lorries, purchased by Clifton Greys in 1931. It is seen here picking up at the B.T.&C.C. coach departure point in Prince Street, probably on Associated Motorways service, and would have been well-used to this type of work, because it came from Black & White Motorways Ltd in 1931. Note the driver stowing luggage on the roof-rack.

A pre-amalgamation shot of Clifton Greys Drivers, including Charlie Bowden, second from the right.

EHY 323. One of the rare German Opel 'Blitz' chassis, with 27-seat Duple body as supplied new to Clifton Greys in 1938

A 2.30pm departure awaiting passengers at Weston-Super-Mare, *c.* 1950. Coaches parked on the seafront 'touted' for business in competition with other operators. Here we have an ex-Clifton Greys 1938 Opel (EHY 798 or 799) offering an afternoon tour to Burrington Combe (for the Rock of Ages) and Cheddar. This would allow the coach to descend the gorge (coaches not allowed since about 1970) and spend about one-and-a-half hours in Cheddar. Time enough for a Somerset Cream Tea (still very popular today), returning at 5.45pm. Fare 4s 9d. To the left and just visible is a Maudsley/Duple of Bakers Coaches, offering a comparable tour to, maybe, Wells & Glastonbury or similar. A coach belonging to WEMS would be not too far away offering another – all home in time for evening dinner.

LHY 432. Daimler CVD6 delivered new to Wessex in 1948 with Duple C33F bodywork, but probably ordered by Clifton Greys. The coach is pictured while parked on a bomb site at St James Square, Bristol, now under the Debenhams store.

"The CLIFTON GREYS" PHONE 34001

ours Start from 15, COLSTON AVE. (& 73, WHITELADIES' ROAD. 10 minutes earlier

Advance Booking Office: DOMINION HOUSE, TRAMWAY CENTRE.

TOUR TO-MORROW (SAT.).— Fare. Bom

2.10 p.m.—RHODODENDRON TOUR: Longleat and Shearwater lake .. 5/- 9. 6

TOURS SUNDAY NEXT, June 18.—

7. 6 a.m.—ABERYSTWYTH and DEVIL'S BRIDGE 15. 18.36
8.30 a.m.—LYNMOUTH, WATERSMEET and EXMOOR 10/6 9.36
8.30 a.m.—Circular Tour: SWANAGE 9/6 9.36
8.30 a.m.—Circular Tour: DORCHESTER and WEYMOUTH ... 9/6 9.34
9. 0 a.m.—Full Loop Tour: WYE VALLEY, Tintern, and CHEPSTOW .. 8/6 9. 6
9. 0 a.m.—WATCHET, BLUE ANCHOR and MINEHEAD 7/6 9. 6
2.30 p.m.—WESTON-SUPER-MARE 2/6 9. 6
1.30 p.m.—Shaftesbury, Zig-Zag, and LARMER TREE ESTATE 7/- 9.45
1.30 p.m.—MINEHEAD 7/- 10. 6

THURSDAY, June 22.—Specially-arranged Coach and Steamer Trip to meet their Majesties the KING and QUEEN on board the Empress of Britain, off the Isle of Wight. Depart 8 a.m. Inclusive Fare, 12

BOOK EARLY — LIMITED ACCOMMODATION.

FOR OTHER AFTERNOON TOURS SEE LISTS.

N.B.—Passengers may be Picked up at Various Points for Sunday Morning Tours

PRIVATE OUTINGS A SPECIALITY. LET US QUOTE YOU.

Prop.: I Fully Insure Against All Risks PHONE:
L. W. ANDREWS. Including Unlimited Liability to Passengers. 34001 (2 lines)

TO-MORROW (SAT.), at 1.30.

ALDERSHOT TATTOO, PHONE 33057/8

10. 6.

Tickets for Reserved Seats from 2. 6. LAST NIGHT.

THURS. Next, 9.0 a.m.—Special Tour to SOUTHAMPTON to witness the return of THEIR MAJESTIES THE KING AND QUEEN from their Canadian and U.S.A. Tour. 9/-; Lunch and Tea included, 3/- extra

AGENTS for ALL MAIN AIR LINES, ASSOCIATED MOTORWAYS, Etc.

Maple Leaf & Maid ALL BRITISH COACHES

Left: An 'advertised tours list' as would have appeared at least twice weekly in one (or both) of the Bristol evening daily papers of the time. This appears to be probably one of the last prior to the outbreak of WWII.

Below: A post-amalgamation picture. A Greys' vehicle on the right and a Morning Star AEC on the left. Left to right the drivers are: Charlie Bowden, George (Dizzie) Stephens, Charlie Murray, George Bascombe, Les Jay, Bill Jay, Bert. Shapcott and an unknown.

Ex-Clifton Greys BV 1739 (again) shown on a sunny day in Brighton. Bill Jay is the driver at the rear, driving GN 4289. Both vehicles are AECs from the early 1930s, re-bodied in 1946 for Clifton Greys.

KHU 823 1947 Daimler CVD6/Plaxton C33F, an ex-Clifton Greys vehicle purchased new. Immediately following is the rebuilt LAE 61.

Psst! Wanna' buy an Opel? – Cheap! EHW 586

such a valuable and sought-after property by 1974. The garage premises were situated in Hampton Road, Redland, but these were vacated in 1948, although they still survive as the headquarters of a painter and decorator business.

In 1938 twelve Opel Blitz chassis with Duple bodies were purchased new; a further six were purchased, second-hand, after the war. This was probably the largest fleet of this type anywhere in Britain. Vehicle imports would indeed have been very rare at that time, but Opel were a General Motors product, and this model was virtually a Bedford WTB with a different grille. All were 27-seaters and were transferred to the new company upon its formation and lasting to *c.* 1954. In common with almost all operators some vehicles were commandeered for the duration of the war but I think I am right in saying that Clifton Greys did not operate through this period and that all vehicles 'not required' were laid up in Hampton Road garage. They appear to have disposed of their 'heavyweights' by the outbreak of hostilities and maybe the 'lightweight' Opels were not required. Being of German origin it may have been thought wiser to keep them locked up. The fleet livery was grey and maroon with dark red trim.

CHAPTER 4

Maple Leaf Garages & Maid of the Mountains

Clifford Whelpton Jordan controlled three fleets. The Maple Leaf Co. had been started as a taxi and garage business in the affluent part of Bristol known as Clifton – not far from Clifton Greys' Whiteladies Road head office. Its premises were at Clifton Road; these remained the main garage premises of Wessex until the end, and, indeed, Wessex National vehicles parked here for a short time until 1975 when the lease expired.

Mr G.J. Jones (Morning Star) and Mr L.W. Andrews (Clifton Greys) jointly purchased C.W. Jordan's interests immediately prior to the formation of Wessex. Cliff Jordan did not take any role in the Wessex operation. He owned several other properties in the area, including a garage repair business at his Queens Road Head Office address, but none of these was included in the sale.

From information available it appears that Mr Jordan, in common with most other operators, also ran a transport business, but it is not known when this would have been established or to what extent. Albert Everett had worked for Cliff Jordan as a fitter/driver since 1923 and, upon the formation of Wessex, decided to retire. Albert's son, Henry, (photographed overleaf) came back from the war, and worked under his father at Maple Leaf, later transferring to Wessex. Henry and Stan Bellamy were jointly responsible for the two complete vehicle rebuilds and the extensive refurbishment programme that took place after the amalgamation. Henry tells me the story of how they were rebuilding Leyland Tiger engines side by side in the workshop at Clifton Road. Stan Bellamy later became Managing Director of Leyland Motors (Australia).

Pre-war and in the period immediately prior to the amalgamation, Cliff Jordan had a fleet of small vans on permanent hire to the Bristol Gas Company Ltd, but, alas, Henry's memory does not go back that far to remember the details. Maple Leaf Motor Coaches was established in 1919 when the first charabancs were introduced. By the 1930s, the fleet had grown to ten vehicles and it appears that Albions were the favoured make, being superseded by Bedford's from 1937 onward. The livery was predominantly blue. Maple Leaf Garages (C.W.Jordan) Ltd, was registered by 1932. In 1934 Mr Jordan purchased the business of the Weston Motor Company fleet from Mr M.G. Moon of Regent Street, Weston, together with the sea front land and properties, providing the firm with a base in the seaside town. This company had been formed in 1909, but at the time of acquisition only two vehicles were in use. The company expanded on this number, and operated as a subsidiary of Maple Leaf until 1939 when its vehicles were requisitioned by The Ministry of War Transport. The company then remained dormant until being absorbed in August 1947 for the purpose of the amalgamation.

In 1938 Mr Jordan took over The Maid of the Mountains Coach Co. Ltd of Wells Road, Bristol. This company was renamed Maid of the Mountains Motor Coach Co. (C.W. Jordan) Ltd, which had been established in 1921 by R.H. & F. Burrows and registered in February 1927. The fleet comprised of various makes up to 1938, but then standardized on Albions and Bedfords as the parent company had done. C.W. Jordan was the only pre-Wessex operator to have used fleet numbers. These were introduced in the early '30s and eventually embraced all three fleets. Having said that, Morning Star used fleet numbers up to the early '30s, but their numbers embodied the goods vehicle fleet also. With the purchase of the Maple Leaf group came the business interests and very valuable property on the seafront at Weston-Super-Mare, Clifton Road Garage and the prestigious Colston Avenue booking-office. In 1952 the seafront property at 10 Beach Road, Weston-Super-Mare, and the licenses based there, were disposed of by Wessex to Bakers Coaches Ltd. Bakers had been established in Weston since they started a passenger-carrying business in 1889 with a pony and trap to taxi people around the town. In 1923 they purchased their first charabanc and painted it red to

A 'young' Henry Everett with Daimler LHY 432 when new (the coach that is …)

Maple Leaf business card.

HT 2853, a 28-seat Dennis of 1921 vintage. This charabanc was licensed to Maid of the Mountains Motor Coach Company Ltd. New in 1921, it was used by this company until 1930. Maid of the Mountains was not taken over by Maple Leaf until 1933.

Maid of the Mountains HT 724 was a 20-seat Daimler from 1921

Similar vehicle HT 726. Now on pneumatic tyres.

MP 3403 was a 1928 Albion 28-seat chara', fleet no. 4.

UM 6371. An Albion PNA 26 with London Lorries body.

HT 726 (see picture above) appears to have been re-bodied by the time that this picture was taken. The vehicle was scrapped in 1942 and possibly ended up as part of a Lancaster Bomber.

FAE 225 was an ex-Maple Leaf 1938 Albion PK115 with Duple C29F bodywork.

FAE 78, the sister vehicle to FAE 225.

operate a Royal Mail contract that they already held. Immediately prior to the outbreak of the Second World War, an office was set up at 16, Beach Road, but this was not used until 1945, when business was resumed. Baker's still occupy the seafront stand, but have since utilised most of the land for residential development. This business is now known as Baker-Dolphin Coaches.

I am informed that ANY coach passing through Cheddar in this period was stopped and photographed. For this the driver received 2s 6d (12.5p), and I imagine that the pictures would have been immediately offered to the proud passengers. Having said that, some photos do appear to have had labels stuck on the originals – maybe these were pictures of the ones that did not stop.

The smaller numbers that you see on the lower side panels of these older vehicles are not to be confused with fleet numbers. These were the numbers issued by the local licensing authority. On the rear of the vehicle would be displayed a large enamel badge giving the name of the local authority in which this vehicle was licensed.

Certificate No. 282955.

THE COMPANIES ACTS, 1929 AND 1947.

COMPANY LIMITED BY SHARES.

SPECIAL AND EXTRAORDINARY RESOLUTIONS

— OF —

MAPLE LEAF GARAGES (C. W. JORDAN)
LIMITED.

Passed 15th day of April, 1948.

At an EXTRAORDINARY GENERAL MEETING of the above-named Company held at Queens Road Garage, Clifton, in the City and County of Bristol, on Thursday the 15th day of April, 1948, the following RESOLUTIONS were passed as SPECIAL and EXTRAORDINARY RESOLUTIONS respectively:—

SPECIAL RESOLUTION.

1. That the Company be wound up voluntarily and that Mr. Herbert Willmott Sydenham Chartered Accountant of 27, Martin Lane, London, E.C.4, be and is hereby appointed Liquidator for the purpose of such winding up.

EXTRAORDINARY RESOLUTION.

2. That the said Liquidator be and is hereby authorised and entitled to exercise any of the powers given by Paragraphs (d), (e) and (f) of Sub-section 1 of Section 191 of the Companies Act, 1929, to a Liquidator in a winding up by the Court.

G. J. JONES,

Chairman.

Maple Leaf winding up order.

CHAPTER 5

Chard & District Motor Services

In March 1949, the fleet of Mrs P. Baulch, t/a Chard & District Motor Services, was acquired. Ten vehicles were involved – nine Bedfords and one Albion – as well as properties and a large yard in the town of Chard, Somerset. The business was owned by Peggy and her husband Jack, and had been set up toward the end of the Second World War. Clarence Herbert 'Jack' Baulch was born in 1916, and, having earlier worked at the Central Motors Garage in the town, he set up his own car sales business at the old Turnpike Garage site on the Honiton road. It was from here that he started Chard and District. He was well known in the town as a Director of Yeovil Town FC. For thirty years he was connected to Chard Town FC, becoming both President and a life member. His family still has transport interests in the town to this day, but in March 1949 the coach business, together with excursion and tour and stage service licences and a portfolio of contracts, was sold to Wessex to give them a foothold in this south Somerset town. Ten vehicles were involved, nine Bedfords of mixed types, OB, OWB, WLB and WTB with bodywork by Mulliner and Duple. A 1937 Albion PK115 was also included. At least three of the Bedfords were "utilities", and the newest vehicle was an OB/Mulliner delivered new in 1949 as a B29F. The types used, as can be seen in the picture below, give the impression that the majority of the work was contract, i.e. schools and workers.

It appears that the original Chard and District Company used fleet numbers.

W.G. Harrison t/a Royal Blue Coaches was the next local company to be acquired, in March 1950. Royal Blue traded from the village of Clapton, and seven vehicles were included in that purchase. Bill Harrison founded his passenger-carrying business in 1924 with a 20cwt Chevrolet fitted with a dual-purpose body when the seats were removed to carry goods. It was the first vehicle in the district to run on pneumatic tyres. There were apparently no side screens to this vehicle, but a fold over canvas roof was fitted. The front seat was a wooden

Chard & District Coaches 1948 in the yard at the former US army camp on Furnham Road.

Three of the Bedford vehicles taken over from the Chard & District fleet. *Left to Right:* JYB 275, a 1948 WLB, HYC 60, a 1947 OB/Duple B26F and DDL 924, a 1946 OB/Duple B31F.

Clarence Herbert 'Jack' Baulch was a local man who made good. Born at Tatworth in 1916, he worked as a motor mechanic at the Central Motors Garage in East Street and went on to start his own car sales business at the old Turnpike Garage on the Honiton road. From there he started the Chard & District Coaches service at the end of the Second World War. A keen sportsman with varied interests, he was best known as a director of Yeovil Town and as chairman of the Perry Street & District Football League from 1967 to 1971. For some thirty years he was connected with Chard Town FC, becoming both its president and a life member.

Chard & District Coaches, *c.* 1947. One of the early coaches with Mr Press at the wheel.

HYC 60. A very smart 1947 Bedford OB/Duple B26F. It appears that the original Chard & District Company used fleet numbers.

bench with the driver sat in the middle and a passenger either side of him. In July 1925 it is recorded that this vehicle once made a three-day trip to London with the Blackdown Women's Institute: a twenty-hour trip to get to London, one day at an exhibition in London and a twenty-hour journey to get home – the only mishap of the journey was a puncture on the first day. Bill Harrison purchased a second coach, a 30cwt Dennis with drop side windows and roll back hood, in 1927. In 1929 a 30cwt Chevrolet came along with a second-hand body attached, to be replaced twelve months later with a new fourteen-seat body by Marks of Wilton, near Salisbury. A daily service was established in 1930 from Crewkerne to Weymouth, but, with the coming of the Road Traffic Act 1930 and the need for all services to be licensed, this service was lost to Southern National only to be won back later on appeal. A 26-seat Bedford was placed in service in 1936 when the aforementioned 1927 Dennis was scrapped. Between 1943 and 1948 the goodwill and licences of several smaller businesses were absorbed by Harrison's. These included Mrs Green of Broadoak, Bonfield's from Bridport and Mr Gear of Charmouth – which included a 1945 Bedford OWB B29F. This vehicle was reported as "very tidy" and made it into the C and D fleet. Harrison's operated the Crewkerne to Weymouth journey mentioned above for many years, and it was later extended beyond Crewkerne to Merriott. May I digress a little and relate the story of Mrs Green and her involvement in the passenger carrying business?

Mrs Green appears to have been a bit of a maverick and is well worth a mention. She had run her business on very thin ice for some years. She ran a farm and also a bus-cum-carrier service from Middle Range Farm in the parish of Whitchurch Canonicorum, assisted by her two sons Ivor and Jimmy. Known as 'The Pride of the Vale', the business started in the 1920s, probably when her husband was alive, and provided a highly individual service. The first bus was a Model T Ford with bodywork by Frank Legg, who was the postmaster, undertaker, cart-, van- and motor-body builder at Long Bredy. On Mondays, Wednesdays, Fridays and Saturdays services ran to Bridport. The terminus in Bridport was the Post Office, where passengers were dropped off, and a visit was made to The Star Inn in West Street to collect parcels. Thursday was the day for Axminster, where Great Markets were held bi-weekly – two buses were needed for this one. On all the routes there was competition from other operators: Herb. Vincent of Thorncombe covered the same route to Bridport and much of the Axminster run, and Bill Harrison and Southern National also ran between Marchwood and Axminster. In addition to the market services, Mrs Green also held school contracts, and, although most of these fitted in with the market service times, there was some overlap. It appears that providing the correct number of vehicles at the given times was a challenge not always met by the intrepid lady.

There were many complaints about the fitness of her vehicles; various warnings were issued, and things usually improved for a short time, but before long the complaints would resume. A 1937 investigation revealed the fact that, although Mrs Green owned six vehicles, only one was licensed for service. Quite how she ran three separate routes to Axminster *and* covered the various school contracts must be a matter for conjecture. Another check revealed an unauthorized vehicle in use, so a school contract was immediately cancelled. Blue Bird of Bridport took over temporarily, but when the new contract was awarded it went to Ivor Green, (Mrs Green's son) who had set up on his own account. Both Ivor and his mother received much adverse comment from head teachers, and, as a result, contracts with both Devon and Dorset County Councils were immediately terminated. Finally Mrs Green was summoned to appear before Bridport Magistrates for having defective tyres, and when the magistrates were told that the vehicle had been carrying schoolchildren they informed the Education Committee, saying that this was not the first time such an offence had been committed. Enough was enough, and the last remaining contract was terminated. Services to Bridport and Axminster continued until they were suspended in 1943, at which time two routes were sold to Bill Harrison. Mrs Green resumed operation after the war had ended, running to Axminster by two different routes on Thursdays and to Bridport from Marshwood every Wednesday and Saturday. By this time she had

GE2427 was a 1929 Leyland Tiger with Cowieson bodywork. The vehicle came with the Harrison business.

Harrison's staff prior to sale of the company. Fortunately we have the names of all those shown in the photograph.
Left to Right: Mr Robertson, Cocoa Bargery, John Lewis, Len Osborne, Bill Harrison, Mrs Forsey, John Obern, Sidney Potterton, Runciman and Henry Ewins.

BFX 992 1945 Bedford OWB came from Harrison's.

The replacement double-decker, HWB 491.

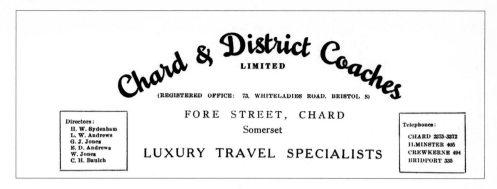

Chard & District Coaches
LIMITED

(REGISTERED OFFICE: 73, WHITELADIES ROAD, BRISTOL 8)

FORE STREET, CHARD
Somerset

LUXURY TRAVEL SPECIALISTS

Directors:
H. W. Sydenham
L. W. Andrews
G. J. Jones
E. D. Andrews
W. Jones
C. H. Baulch

Telephones:
CHARD 2375-3372
ILMINSTER 405
CREWKERNE 404
BRIDPORT 335

The original company letter-heading after the takeover. Note that a member of the Baulch family retained a seat on the board, although this was most likely a procedural move.

moved her operation to Broad Oak. In 1949 Mrs Green sold the business to Chard & District, by now owned by Wessex. Thus passed a woman who ran a highly individual service, and perhaps epitomized the phrase "independent Operator".

Back to Harrison's. In 1948 Bill Harrison had been granted permission to operate a double-decked vehicle on the service from Crewkerne to Weymouth, and purchased a 1929 Leyland TD1 with a Cowieson body from Glasgow Corporation for the purpose. The service was also extended to run from Merriott. This vehicle was among the vehicles transferred to C&D, but was never licensed by them. It was sold for scrap in 1950. A replacement decker was obtained from Sheffield Corporation in 1954 in the shape of a "utility" Daimler CWA6, to maintain the Weymouth service. HWB 491 became the first decker to be owned and operated by the parent or subsidiary company.

In January 1954 a new operating company was registered in the name of Wessex Motorways (Bristol) Ltd, and at that time twenty-one vehicles were transferred to the new company. Len Osborne, who I met on a few occasions and found to be a gentleman, became Manager of this new company.

Vehicles added to the fleet from Bristol remained painted in the familiar red and grey Wessex colours of the time, and so allowed movement of vehicles from one to the other. Some vehicles were purchased directly by Chard & District MS, or the later company, and remained licensed to them, but details of these have been included in the later whole fleet analysis as it would be difficult to do otherwise. Vehicles were moved backwards and forwards between Bristol and Chard and vice versa, but in each case a change of ownership would need to have been notified to the licensing authority. The licensing authority would need to have been notified about ownership, and the legal ownership transfers changed on the side of the vehicle. The fleetname "Wessex" appeared on every front and back glass on every coach – the name on the back doors, applied by transfer, read (after 1954) Wessex Motorways (Bristol) Ltd or Wessex Coaches Ltd, Bristol, on vehicles transferred from Bristol.

The business of S.J. Wakley of Axminster was purchased in January 1960. Three vehicles were involved, a Bedford OWB, a Maudlslay Marathon and an AEC, but all were disposed of very quickly, though the AEC was only ten years old, in very good condition and befitting the (Wessex) company profile at the time. The history of this company has been very well documented locally by Roger Grimley. As a boy, Stan Wakley had helped his father to deliver newspapers around the district. Obliged to cease his previous employment working on the farm due to an argument with a threshing machine, which caused him to lose an arm, Joseph Wakley bought himself a donkey and cart to collect the papers from Axminster Station each day for distribution. Alas, at the relatively young age of forty-five Joseph died of pneumonia, leaving Stanley to fend for himself.

Stan was determined to make something of himself, and having learnt much of the geography of the district with his father and noticed the lack of motor cars thereabouts, he envisaged a need for motor transport locally. In 1927, at the age of sixteen, Stan borrowed thirty-eight pounds from his mother and set off for London to buy a motor car. Being only sixteen, when the legal age for driving was seventeen, he was forced to take a friend with him to drive home. After being a little 'inaccurate' with his age Stan got himself a licence. But time was not on his side, so his friend gave him some basic lessons. That day they jacked the rear wheels of the car off the ground to enable him to 'drive' and get some gear change practice. The reason for the urgency was that he had been booked to take a passenger to Exeter hospital the very next day – 25 miles away. Some journey for a sixteen-year-old boy who had never driven until the day before. Stan's foresight was rewarded, and the business prospered.

His car became an essential part of village life, and was hired by both the local District Nurse and the Midwife at the hospital whenever either was required to attend a home visit. The Devon Constabulary hired Stan's taxi on a regular basis to take the local 'bobby' to Axminster Police Station, and he was also called upon if anyone was arrested in nearby Membury. Neither the parish of Membury nor Stockland had ever enjoyed a bus service, and few people had their own transport, so market days in nearby towns meant that Stan was kept busy shuttling back and forth all day. This led him to thinking that if he bought a bus he could take all the people in one journey, saving them expense and offering a much better service. Off he went to London again and bought a three-year-old fourteen-seat Ford registered GF8503 for £60. This was now 1933.

The next few years saw business continue to expand, with services to the towns on market days and excursions to the races, Honiton Fair, Exeter

Pantomime. During the summer there were half-a-crown trips to the seaside at Seaton. Private hire enquiries and bookings were coming in from a wide area – all wanting to travel on 'The Rambler'. One service that Stan provided was the charging of accumulator batteries as used in early radios. A tray was fitted to the floor of the bus next to the driver into which the charged batteries were placed at the start of the journey, and, as the bus ambled along, people would come out of their houses to exchange their "dead" accumulators for a charged one at *6d* a time – a nice little sideline. Imagine that today for the 'elf and safety gang.

In 1937 a new school opened in Axminster and tenders were invited for the supply of transport. Six buses per day were required. Stan thought that he might at least get one of them; but, to his utter amazement, he was awarded contracts for three buses per day. What made the shock even greater was that at that time he only owned the one bus, so off to London again. He managed to find three buses to suit the purpose: a 1930 Chevrolet for the Membury run earning 17s 6d a day, an eight-year-old twenty-seat Reo for the Dalwood and Kilmington contract at 22s a day, and, finally, a large Gilford for Chardstock at 26s a day. Staff had to be engaged for these buses: Len Cornish joined Stan from Southern National as a driver/mechanic at a wage of £2 a week, and others employed in the farming community were recruited to drive part-time. While all of this was happening, Stan had opened Shrubbery Garage and Petrol Sales, with a cafe behind on the main A35 in Axminster. He later gained a Commer agency and a showroom was built on the original site. World War Two brought volumes of work, within the constraints of the fuel allowance. Evacuees were collected from Axminster station and delivered to their allotted billets in the villages. Passengers were crammed into buses for the journey to Axminster; when full, the buses doubled back to collect those left behind. More school journeys came through, and one contract had to be given to another operator. After the war newer coaches were purchased, enabling a programme of excursions and tours to be operated.

Stan was approached to sell the bus and coach side of the business, and this he did, to Wessex Motorways on 1 January 1960. Wessex were no doubt very keen to get hold of the extensive list of contracts that Stan now held, as well as his Private Hire business and Excursion and Tours licences, express service licences from Honiton and stage-carriage licences. There were two of the latter: from Stockland to Honiton and from Webble Green to Axminster. These would effectively dovetail into those already held. The latter two service licences passed to Seward of Dalwood in 1967. Somewhere along the way the licences (only) were also taken over from Love of Chard, Sully's Coaches of Chard, Vincent's of Thorncombe and Victory Coaches of Horton.

By 1973 it appears that the Wessex Motorways company was run down, and vehicle stock was transferred back to the main fleet at Bristol. The stage

Stan Wakley's fleet lined up at Axminster *c.* 1948.

BEA 707 was a 1944 Duple-bodied Bedford OWB acquired from P. Baulch. This one passed back to Bristol for two years before being disposed of in 1952.

service licences were transferred to Southern National, while the Excursions and Tours went mainly to Taylor's of Tintinhull. The contract fleet, as explained in a later chapter, had been very reliant on facilities at Chard during its entire life. However, by the late '60s it tended to be self-sufficient at whichever power station it was attached to, and continued to be so until the final contract ended at Heysham, Lancs., in 1976.

We have seen above that Chard and District, and the later Wessex Motorways, primarily traded on a very large portfolio of contract workings, which could easily exist with a lower quality fleet of older vehicles and the employment of part-time drivers. More modern vehicles – but not new ones – were later placed into the fleet to encourage summer visitors to partake in the daily tours programme provided by the company. I think that it can be fairly said that, although Wessex did little to update the ages of the vehicles based here, they at least vastly improved the standard of the vehicles at Chard.

The Bedfords were taken over with the fleets of Chard & District and Harrison's did not last very long, although three (CUJ 656 and 658 as well as KYB 568) did make it into the Motorways fleet in 1954, where they lasted until 1956. During the later 1950s and early 1960s, the fleet consisted mainly of AECs and Daimlers, with bodywork by any one of about eight different manufactures, built on chassis that were anything up to fifteen years old. The drivers kept these coaches in immaculate condition both inside and out. Those old coaches were a real credit to the Chard Drivers, and in the summer both coach and driver were worked very hard. For most of the season, certainly from Whitsun to September, those vehicles worked seven days a week: on the school and workers contracts, on Private Hire within the Chard, Axminster and Bridport areas, on the advertised tours that were operated by Chard & District, and finally from late Fridays they were employed on whatever weekend Express work that was required of them. These journeys could take them to any corner of Southern England on Associated Motorways work, although it would normally be to London or Birmingham. They could even have been brought to Bristol at weekends to operate our own tours or period bookings.

Immediately after finishing their school contracts, the drivers would, on a Friday afternoon, each make their way to Bristol and park in the yard at Kingswood to sleep overnight in their vehicles ready for the off early on Saturday morning. Schedules were usually arranged that enabled Chard drivers to return from say, Victoria or Birmingham to Torquay or Plymouth, and then to make their way home empty, but this was not always possible. Thus they would spend a second night on the back seat of the coach somewhere away from home in readiness for a Sunday duty – and it was not unknown for the third night to be so spent also. I remember those drivers as a cheery lot, and nothing was too

These pages: A selection of the Chard-based vehicles that I would have encountered at Kingswood *c.* 1964.

much trouble for them. They were mainly older men, in their fifties and sixties, probably from farming stock in their native Devon or Dorset, and quite used to the long hours. We used to leave the office unlocked overnight when they were present at Kingswood to allow them to use all the facilities, and to make themselves a cup of tea.

There was one incident that I recall at this time. Raymond and his family lived above the office at Kingswood. He had a pet dog which also doubled as the guard dog – quite handy really, because Kingswood garage was an unfenced property directly off Moravian Road. Ray used to let the dog out last thing at night and 'Snowy' used to enjoy chasing the courting couples off the site. He knew all of our drivers so, if one happened to be still in the garage and called the dog by name, he was at least sixty per cent safe – oh yes, 'Snowy' could be quite fierce. He chased a Chard driver that he did not recognise one night and bit him.

At the end of the 1965 season, all of the SAEs 38-seaters were transferred to Chard, together with a couple of ex-Feltham's 41s, followed in '67 by one ex Feltham 41 seater and the four UAEs 1955 38-seaters. At the end of 1967 the rest of the Feltham's 41-seaters emigrated also, along with THR 240 and 821 CUP. In 1969, when ten years old, the entire DHY batch of Super Vegas were transferred, together with the other second-hand acquisitions, 157 ALH and 6964 NU. The fleet must have appeared much more up-to-date at that time, if only to the local enthusiasts. Most of the older Chard coaches were transferred back to the main fleet at this time, meaning that the vehicles concerned were being either sold to dealers or moved on to the contract sites. It will be noted here that all second-hand Bedford acquisitions were now based at Chard.

A mixed batch of Bedford SBs numbered THR 240, 821 CUP, 973 DHY, 6469 NU and 486 CRO were transferred back from Chard and withdrawn from ownership and use by Wessex Motorways in December 1973. They were re-licensed to the main fleet and transferred to the Heysham contract. It appears that these vehicles were the very last coaches to have been licensed to Wessex Motorways before that company was wound up. Although much use was made of Chard facilities for the whole life of the Contract vehicles, the Contract fleet was at all times in the legal ownership of Wessex Coaches, with the legal address on the side of the bus being shown as 73 Whiteladies Road.

CHAPTER 6

Kingswood Queen

On 1 January 1961, the Kingswood Queen fleet of G.F. Feltham & Sons was purchased, along with sixteen vehicles. This is the company with which I am most familiar, and which must be the oldest of all of these constituents.

Feltham's passenger-carrying roots can be traced back to the very early 1900s. The business was founded as a coal merchant by Harriett 'Grandma' Feltham around 1883. Mrs Feltham was widowed and left to bring up five young children at the age of forty-four. There were no government handouts in those days, so at first she chopped firewood, which was then delivered to people's houses, to earn the money to feed her children. Later she acquired a donkey, enabling her to go to Speedwell pit to collect coal in a sack on the donkey's back. She would deliver the coal with the firewood on a hand-cart from a yard in Bank Road, Kingswood. I understand that this yard was also used by the travelling shows featuring boxing booths and coconut shies. Business prospered, and she went on to a donkey and cart and later to a horse and cart. Harriet died in 1908 at the age of (?) sixty-three. Only one son carried on the business – Gilbert, who was born in January 1879, left school to work for his mother, later buying the horse and other effects from her prior to her death. Gilbert then bought a wagonette and another larger horse, enabling him to take parties out at weekends. The passenger traffic had begun. Another son who had planned to join the business was killed in the First World War. Gilbert bought more horses to hire out to whomever needed them. In 1908 Gilbert purchased property at 82 Moravian Road, allowing a much larger coal yard where he could build stables and a brake and carriage shed. Harriet Feltham died the day after the family moved to this address.

Gilbert married, having three sons and a daughter; he passed away in 1939. The sons, Walter, Reginald and Albert, each became involved in the business from an early age. Walter was fourteen years older than his youngest sibling,

Albert, and before he was twelve years of age he was an accomplished lad with the horses. His father had about twelve horses by then and had acquired a four-horse brake which could carry thirty passengers. He also had a landau, which could be pulled by a pair of black horses for funerals or a pair of bays for the first-class customers. With a modification of the shafts, this rubber-tyred landau could also be used with a single horse or as a carriage and pair. Apparently, it was very popular for trips to Bath Races. With two horses up the passengers did not have to walk up the steep hill to the course at Lansdowne, near Bath. Young Walter could handle all types of horses and wagons, and had given up school by the age of twelve. In about 1925 Gilbert had purchased a house and land at 99 Staple Hill Road, Fishponds. I remember coaches being parked on these premises during the war. This became the home of Walter where he brought up his family. The property was disposed of during the 1950s. I visited this house whilst doing my research for this article to find that, although it is nowadays used as a builders' merchant's yard, the large garage, complete with the 'pit', still remains at the rear.

The main garage and offices situated at 82 Moravian Road lasted for many years, but were relinquished mid-'50s, when the land at No. 54 was purchased and developed. No. 82 was given up, and later became part of Lucas Ruskit mills. Further up Moravian Road lived Reg and his family in a house adjoining land at No. 54, and the boys purchased a plot of land lower down, having a

This well-loaded combination appears to be starting a Private Hire from Barton Hill, Bristol.

This page: Father and three sons – The Felthams

Phone Nos.
Kingswood 81
Fishponds 263

G. Feltham & Sons,

Charabanc Proprietors and Haulage Contractors,

82 MORAVIAN ROAD, KINGSWOOD, BRISTOL
AND
99 STAPLE HILL RD., FISHPONDS, BRISTOL.

Harriet Feltham

This is probably the 30-seater brake, that Walter speaks of, with four horses in hand.

FROM one donkey cart to 24 luxury motor coaches. That's the rate at which the Kingswood firm of G. Feltham and Sons, Ltd., has rocketed to fame in 60 years. Now the firm—one of the oldest pasenger-carrying firms in the West Country—proudly announces the opening of its new Coach Station in Moravian-road, Kingswood.

The station has a garage to hold 24 coaches, its own set of petrol pumps, a streamlined block of offices and waiting room complete with cloakrooms for 35 passengers.

It was more than 60 years ago that a harassed Kingswood woman was left to look after her seven children. Her husband had died while they were all young. Somehow they had to be fed. It was then that the idea of hauling coal with a donkey-cart came to "Grandma" Feltham.

Business progressed and a pony and cart was the next move. From there a wagonette and horse came easily and the first passenger traffic began. Only one son carried on the business— Mr G. Feltham. A brother who planned to be in the firm was killed during the first world war. Despite this setback and the shortage of men and horses during the first world war, besides the fact that the vehicles were requisitioned, the firm got back on its feet again.

Between the two wars the hauling business was once again introduced and the firm went on from strength to strength. But another serious setback was still to come. Nationalisation of the haulage business was a big blow in 1947, to the firm.

However, the present three directors, Mr Reginald Feltham, Mr Albert Feltham and Mr Walter Feltham—all grandsons of the original woman with the donkey cart—decided to concentrate on the passenger side of the business.

Soon Moravian-road became a crowded centre on Bank Holidays and weekends. With the relaxation of controls coach tours and holiday travel boomed. The original property became too congested. Passengers had to wait on the roadside and pavements—a danger to other traffic. And the need of a proper coach station was soon realised.

Now with this new station there will be even more comfort for the vast numbers of people who use the coaches in this modern fleet. For in the winter, nearly as much as summer the firm is kept busy on works outings to London and weekend football parties.

Besides the private hire, there are daily excursions to all the popular resorts and express services to Brighton, Worthing, Southsea, Bournemouth, Weymouth, Seaton, Sidmouth, Exmouth, Teignmouth, Torquay and Paignton during the holiday season with numerous picking-up points covering the whole of East Bristol.

Above and right:
From the *Bristol Evening World*,
November 1958.

This picture represents what I believe to be the very first motorised passenger vehicle owned by Feltham's, registered AD9563 and with Reg driving. This vehicle is not listed in the fleet history but appears to be the 14-seater Model T Ford bought for Walter by his father *c*. 1916 for the sum of £800. Walter practised his driving for two hours on this vehicle when new before taking a party to Weston from the Gospel Hall at Staple Hill.

The vehicle is L9267, a 1922 Nofiat[?] 20-seater which was on of the very early passenger vehicles owned by Feltham's. As usual, Walter is the driver.

Walter with HW 1633, an Albion PNA26 30-seater from 1928.

DF 7729 1929 26-seater Albion PKC26 with Reg.

A fine picture of the line-up for the 1946 annual outing to Bournemouth of T. Miles & Co. which was a boot and shoe manufacturer in Soundwell Road, Kingswood, Bristol. Albert Feltham is to the front right of the picture with a Duple-bodied 1936 Leyland Cub (DYK325) and is followed by four wartime Bedford OWBs, (HHY 67, JAE 4, EDG855 & FAD412) the last of which is driven by George Bateman. Behind George is a Dennis Ace (YD 8337 or 9926) with Stan Peacock, and, on the pavement, a pre-war Dennis Lancet (EN 5449).

Felthams' drivers *c.* 1950 outside of Walter's house, Lewington road, Fishponds. *Back row Left to Right:* Len Machin, Stan Peacock, Albert Feltham, Bill Liddington Jnr, [unknown], [unknown]. *Front row Left to Right:* [unknown], [unknown], Walter Feltham, George Bateman, Dick Withey & Ted Jefferies.

1947 Whitson-bodied AEC Regal.

A large Private Hire job, Anchor Road

PHT 164 was an Albion FT39AN with a Longwell Green C31F body. It was new in 1952 and lasted four years.

NHW 479 1951 Leyland PSU/1 (Royal Tiger) with Longwell Green C41C bodywork. Feltham's had two of these

MHT 52 was a Leyland CPO2 (Comet) with Longwell Green C35F body. This vehicle was one of the six Comets owned by Feltham's, two of which came in second-hand.

967 BHU 1958 SB, later converted to SBO. The vehicle passed to Wessex in 1961 and was driven by George Bateman from new until about 1964.

bungalow built in the rank for their mother, who died in 1958. A large aircraft hangar was purchased and erected to the rear of the yard at No. 54 to house the fleet. Kingswood Queen vehicles were painted in two shades of blue with a primrose yellow flash and window surrounds.

By 1961 I had married, and was living not very far from Moravian Road and Feltham's depot, so I saw their vehicles quite often. It was on 1 January 1961 that Wessex took control of the business. At the time of the takeover Bedford vehicles dominated the fleet, but this had not always been the case. Not too many years previous, they had owned a magnificent fleet, mainly of Leylands but including one Albion, and prior to 1955 had AECs, a post-war Dennis Lancet and a few OBs among their Leylands. It would have been at this time that they also operated six Leyland Comets and were the largest operator of this type in the area, and indeed the whole of Bristol. Although not exclusively, they generally favoured Longwell Green bodies on their new vehicles in the early '50s, as this builder was situated only three miles away. Longwell Green had a lot of patronage locally, and their products could be found in most of the local fleets. The majority of Feltham's early '50s fleet came in new, but there were second-hand purchases in between.

In 1956 No. 54 was extended and modern facilities were built, including a single-storey booking office and waiting room. A full-page advertisement was taken in the *Bristol Evening World* in 1958 to publicise the event, and is reproduced below. In 1961 the building was further extended by Wessex to include an upper floor and residential accommodation. Walter, Reg and Albert remained directors until 31 December 1960. Reg continued to live in the property adjoining the garage in Moravian Road, and Albert lived in the bungalow at the rear of the premises in Derrick Road. Sixteen vehicles were taken over by Wessex. Four of these were never operated and were sold immediately, leaving twelve. One was a 38-seat Duple Vega, nine were 41-seat Vegas and two were 41-seaters (Plaxton bodied), one of which carried a Consort body (YHT 810) and the other (560 BHU) was a later Embassy. Most of the vehicles were converted to diesel power by the end of the 1961 season, but I personally used YHY 370 with a petrol engine on Easter Monday 1962, so one or two vehicles did run a little late before conversion.

CHAPTER 7

Renown Coaches

In 1965 the licences of A.Burchill t/a Renown Coaches of Broad Street, Staple Hill, were transferred to Wessex. Arthur had several school contracts with Chipping Sodbury Grammar and Rodway Schools. His coaches were always immaculate and painted silver and a very light blue. I recall that one of his coaches was the first that I ever saw fully carpeted – that would have been a luxury in the '60s. He also had a portfolio of good class private-hire customers. We would sometimes run on hire to Renown, covering morning and afternoon schools work, and Arthur would be at the pick up point making sure that the children behaved themselves and did no damage to his vehicles. I remember driving one of his coaches on Sodbury school run one day and him giving me strict instructions that if any of the children misbehaved, they were to be put off the bus and made to walk home – imagine that today! The four drivers employed full-time in 1965 were all quite elderly. They came to Wessex, but three moved on to S.G. Wiltshire's (Princess Mary) within a very short time, and I think the other one retired. I remember these three names as Jack Bateman, Bill Boulton and his brother, Albert. They used to come to work dressed in dark suits and looking more like funeral directors, but, as drivers went in the mid-sixties, these three really were the best and most professional. No vehicles were involved in the take-over.

Oliver Burchill had started this business, which was to become Renown Coaches, in the 1870s, when he bought a pony and trap to deliver milk. He was later joined by his brother William, and the business prospered. Their father was an engineer at the local pit and died fairly early in life, but their mother was a tower of strength, and it was she who decided what the boys should do. From the pony and trap, the business progressed to trolleys with two horses. Much work was done for the council, although the competition was keen and rates low. The business continued to expand and the brothers bought two-hand and four-hand brakes, as well as one- and two-horse carriages for hire. At the turn of the century, the partnership was dissolved – William bought out his brother. Until this time, the brothers had traded

Burchill's early four-in-hand Brake.

DD 1269 was a Crossley of 1922 vintage.

The site of Burchill's garage in Broad Street, Staple Hill, 1915. The young lad is probably Arthur Burchill himself. It must have been one of the very first petrol outlets.

TR 3901 was an Albion but I have no history for this vehicle.

Arthur sold KDD 389 in 1960, having owned it from new in 1950. So impressed was the new owner with the livery and the name (Renown) that he asked if he could keep it as it was. It was a Leyland PS1.

Arthur Burchill's flagship, new in 1955 and an entrant in that year's Brighton Coach Rally was PDF 603, a magnificent AEC Duple Elizabethan C41C-bodied vehicle. The first under-floor engined vehicle for the company, I can vouch for the fact that it was still in this condition when disposed of in 1962 and probably driven by Jack Bateman throughout its time with Renown.

from Ducie Road in Staple Hill, Bristol, but William bought houses and land at 72 and 74 Broad Street, Staple Hill, and it was from here that the business operated for the next sixty-five years. Jones Brothers of Kingswood built the brakes that Burchill bought, with a four-horse brake costing between £150 and £200. The four-horse brake required a man at the rear to operate the wheel brakes; he would also feed and care for the horses when stopped during a journey. The passengers sat facing each other with room for luggage at their feet. For weather protection, a folding waterproof cover was erected on metal standards that slotted into brackets on the side of the carriage. This cover was marketed as 'A One Man Hood', but I am told that it needed about eight men to erect it, and that was when the passengers would be called upon to assist.

It was later that a similar vehicle was introduced into this country from France; the main difference was that the seats were set across the body of the vehicles and passengers sat facing the front. This was known as a char-à-banc. Motor coaches were introduced after the First World War, the first two were fourteen-seater Crossleys, followed by a succession of Fords, Guys and Albions (mostly purchased new) between the wars. A very mixed bag of Albion, Bedford, Leyland, a couple of AECs (and a Foden in there somewhere also) come, after WWII. Bodybuilders were also very mixed: Plaxton, Duple, Gurney Nutting, Harrington and Burlingham made up the post WWII fleet. Arthur would have, I imagine, come into the business in about 1920. He succeeded his father William, but he certainly did not appear to have much of a vehicle-buying policy. At their peak, Renown operated about twelve coaches and employed ten drivers, but by 1965 the fleet had been run down to three or four, which Arthur sold off privately. The licences for his excursions and tours were transferred to Wessex. It was at that time that Arthur slipped off quietly to enjoy his retirement near Bournemouth. William had chosen the title 'Renown' Coaches after the famous First World War battleship.

CHAPTER 8

The Vehicles

We know that essential services had to be maintained throughout the war period. Nationally, children had to be moved to railway stations for the purpose of evacuation. I personally recall being taken by my parents to Alexandra Park School at Fishponds, and from there travelling by a Queen of the Road coach to Stapleton Road Station for a train to Halwill Junction in Devon. I believe that this would have been in 1942. I was only away for six weeks, as a stray bomb landed in the field near where I was staying. My mother said that if I was to be killed she would rather it be in Bristol than in Devon, so she came to fetch me home. I was told that huge numbers of coaches were required, at the time of the Dunkirk evacuation, to ferry troops from the Channel ports to every corner of the UK, and in our local area to Eastville Park, where a tented city was formed.

Throughout the war period troops were moved between camps, particularly around the Salisbury Plain area, and later South Devon at the time leading up to D-day in 1944. In our local area, thousands of people would have needed transport several times a day (and night) to and from Bristol Aeroplane Company's Filton works. Munitions factories abounded in the Bristol area and nearby at Yate. Some buses and coaches were destroyed by enemy action, putting further strain on already depleted stocks. Added to that, schoolchildren still needed to be transported to and from school. All of this would have kept all local coach operators very busy. I recall that we saw little of my own father at this time as Bristol Tramways were also carrying these personnel. All this on top of maintaining the regular bus services in the town and country areas.

We also know from the records that some operators were allocated new vehicles in the shape of the Bedford OWBs to allow them to carry out these duties. The Bedford OWB was certainly built to austerity standards – the most obvious being wooden seats. Morning Star had three such vehicles between 1942 and 1943. In 1943, the cost to an operator of a Bedford OWB 32 seater was £810. They were painted brown; the chassis would have been brand new, although many parts that would otherwise have been made of cast alloys now had to make do with cast iron instead. The bodywork was invariably by Duple (though not entirely), providing seated accommodation for thirty-two passengers on wooden slatted seats with little legroom for each. The body was single-skinned and the roof got so warm on a hot day that you could burn your hand on it. There were only two half-drop opening windows, one each side so airflow was very restricted. Even driving with the folding entrance door open on a hot summer's day would not have stopped the atmosphere becoming very oppressive; one could have fried an egg on the roof at the height of summer. In winter, condensation formed inside the roof and dripped onto the passengers below. I read somewhere that such a vehicle was being used for a 'pub' outing to The Derby, (after the war) and still retaining the wooden seats. After a couple of hours the driver noticed that a lot of the passengers were standing and, upon asking the organiser what the problem was, he was told that they were "giving their backsides a rest". I know that Morning Star in particular ran a twice-weekly service from Bristol to Winsley Sanatorium, near Bradford-on-Avon, throughout the period of the war – this being a TB isolation hospital and that is probably part of the reason why they were allocated their three utility vehicles.

Many articles have been written on the subject of wartime buses, the detail of which is not warranted here other than to mention a few facts concerning the Bedford OWB. Suffice it to say that 2,841 Bedford OWBs were built for civilian use up to the end of production in September 1945. Most were bodied by Duple, although 800 were completed by other builders to an identical specification. Here was a fairly robust little vehicle weighing about 3 tons 15cwt complete, powered by a 27hp petrol engine returning about 10mpg, compared to a typical heavy-duty single-decker weighing in at about 6 tons and returning lower mpg figures, albeit on diesel fuel. Another advantage of the OWB, with so many drivers being away at the war, was that it made an ideal vehicle for women to drive, and many were employed to do so. Applications for any type of wartime bus from 1941 onwards were a matter of obtaining Ministry of War Transport approval, with the operator having to show the need to meet public bus service or worker contract transport requirements. The operator had to accept whatever make of vehicle and body was forthcoming, although Bedford was the only single-deck choice that would have been available in single deck form. There were slightly more options with double-deckers. Only a minority of the major fleets took OWBs into stock, and those that did operated them mainly in rural areas. BT & CC took fifty-five in 1942-3 and kept some for as long as seven years in their austerity form. All were delivered in khaki livery and repainted into operators' colours as soon as possible. After the war, many OWBs were modernised and updated. Some were re-bodied to the luxury specification of the time, and passed into fleets for several years' further work as front-line vehicles.

Clifton Greys retained its unique fleet of Opels, ironically model-named 'Blitz'. Twelve had been purchased new in 1939, and further numbers were added second-hand after the war. As the chassis were of German origin, I think that they may have been hard to sell; but, even more likely, I suppose that it would have not been a popular move to use them with the political feeling of the time. I have learned that, certainly initially, the Ministry of War Transport, (as it was known after 1939), requisitioned only heavyweight vehicles less than two years old, although this ruling must have been extended to include older vehicles later. There are isolated instances of vehicles being requisitioned prior to 1939, but I can find no procedural evidence to support any regulations of the time. Many buses and coaches were commandeered in the early days and kept in strategic places, so that people could be evacuated quickly in the event of an invasion by foreign forces. I was told a story that Bill Jones was delivering with a lorry in London towards the end of the war, and he came across a compound within Regents Park containing a large number of passenger vehicles. Upon further investigation, he found some Morning Star vehicles that had been parked here for the duration. Negotiations began, and those vehicles were released back to Morning Star. I wonder if these were the three Leyland Tigers previously mentioned, and were returned from The Navy in July 1944.

Vehicles, whether with the ministry or not, were worked hard and to capacity. Driving tests for bus drivers were suspended during the war, and those new to the job were granted a driver's permit on the recommendation of their employer. Drivers' hours' regulations were relaxed to the point of non-existence, and, with all of these points combined, vehicles (and drivers) were driven into the ground. In some cases vehicles had to be laid-up, as the owners could not obtain suitable spare-parts when needed. This situation became so dire that the ministry introduced a system whereby priority permits were issued giving the owner first call on any spares that were available. This did not solve the problem, and it was sometimes necessary to wait until enough requests had been entered for a certain part to justify the manufacture of a batch. These parts would have been made from whatever suitable materials were available.

At the end of the war vehicles were returned, some direct to the owners, and some to dealers, the numbers of whom were growing overnight. Operators were compensated for the loss of use of their vehicles. Some operators had gone out of business or for whatever reason did not want their vehicles returned, and these were duly compensated. The prices of the second-hand vehicles rocketed. I read of an instance whereby in 1947, a 27-seat Austin with very high mileage and soon to need a new engine, gearbox and rear axle, was sold to an operator for the sum of £3,500 by Arlington Coach Sales of London. It had cost £1,600 when new in 1939. Operators set about modernising their charges. As far as the OWBs were concerned, it was not difficult to replace the wooden seats with a 'new' set from a redundant vehicle, give the vehicle a smart new repaint, reduce the seating capacity to maybe twenty-seven and to fit more opening windows. Many were completely rebodied. New engines were fitted, pre-war petrol-engined vehicles were converted to 'oilers' by the fitment of Perkins P6 units. Coaches were sent away to coachbuilders to be re-bodied by the huge number of companies that had sprung up for the purpose. In some cases operators combined their resources and set up their own builders: Transun springs to mind, owned by a consortium of Lancashire operators and headed by Yelloway. The thought behind this move was probably due to the long lead times being quoted for either rebuilds or new vehicles. Some smaller operators who had put their names down in 1946 for an OB took delivery in 1951 – at the time that the SB had been announced.

So, Wessex came into full operational existence in 1948, and it must be remembered that 1948 was a year of continued deprivation. Added to this was the threat of transport nationalisation. Henry Russet's Royal Blue was a typical local example – their lorries had been taken over by the newly formed Road Transport Executive, of which British Road Services was a part, and their coaches passed to Bristol Tramways, itself part of the Tilling group. This topic must certainly have been the talk of any people in the position that Mr Jones and Mr Andrews were contemplating. The lorries belonging to E. Jones & Sons Ltd had in fact passed to Pioneer Transport the previous year, and this was one of the first fleets in the Bristol area to go to BRS. The average family certainly did not own a car – and even if they did petrol was still on ration so they would not have travelled very far. People had endured and were still recovering from six years of war, not being able to move far from the end of their own street, let alone to visit a seaside resort. So they would have been only to pleased to get away – maybe for just a day or, if they could afford it, to go to the seaside for longer. To travel twenty miles from Bristol to Weston-Super-Mare must have been an absolute luxury – even riding in the back of a dust-cart if necessary.

I remember the queues of people and the lines of double-decker buses, both inside and outside of the Beach Bus Station at Weston, waiting to return them to Bristol. I understand that both Wessex and many other operators ran tours with the wartime OWBs, the wooden seats still in situ in the early days after the war, such was the demand. Not only petrol, of course, which remained on ration until 1950, but also all foodstuffs would still have been rationed. I recall being taken to Clevedon on the bus with my younger brother and sister shortly after the war ended. We visited a small café and ordered tea for the family. I think I had two very thin slices of bread, butter and jam and asked for more, but was unable to have more because that was the ration. So maybe it was not just the ride: it was a chance to eat out and eke out their rations at home. I started my employment at Cathedral Garage in 1951, and recall one particular Saturday morning when a line of coaches stretched from the Hotwell Road end of Anchor Road, past our workshop entrance and as far as one could see in the direction of the Tramways Centre. I could not now hazard a guess as to how many vehicles were in that line – but Anchor Road is half a mile long at least.

Because of the austerities, coach companies were kept very busy. There was a huge boom in passenger numbers. They coped, within the limitations of their own fuel allocations, although I cannot say how this worked. I know that as late as 1962, when I joined Wessex, one of my first tasks was to update the returns to the Ministry of Transport whereby every journey by every vehicle had to be documented for the previous year together with mileages covered, the number of passengers carried and a passenger per seat/mile figure calculated. I believe that this was the continuation of immediate post-war records to justify vehicle usage. People wanted to get away to anywhere, and the vehicles had to be provided to cater for them.

As I have said, waiting lists for new vehicles were stretched; materials were hard to come by, and were not of the highest standards. Records show that several vehicles re-bodied *c.*1946 had to be rebuilt again *c.*1951 as the timber frames had rotted in that very short time.

LHY 431 was one of the two complete Wessex rebuilds (as already mentioned) it also received a new registration. This was a reconstruction of a 1936 AEC Regal, which had originated in Aberdeen and was acquired through the War Department. It had an AEC 7.7-litre oil engine. Disposed of by Wessex in 1952, it passed through several owners and was last licensed in August 1967.

ANALYSIS OF VEHICLE PURCHASES 1947 TO 1973

S/H Vehicles Acquisition Vehicles

Year	D/D	Coach	New	Totals	
1947		76		76	From constituent companies upon formation – HY 748 was never operated so the figure was actually 75.
1948			6	6	4 OBs, 1 Daimler, 1 Albion
1949			13	13	10 OBs, 2 Daimlers, 1 AEC – all new but incl. 1 rebuild.
1950			10	10	From Chard & District
1950			3	3	3 New Bedford OBs
1950		7	7	5	7 Bedford OBs, 2 Leylands ex-Harrison's
1951	1		1		1 s/h Bedford WTB
1952			6	6	6 new Bedford SBs
1952		5		4	4 Bedford OBs and 1 Leyland
1953		6		6	4 Bedford OBs, 2 Leylands
1954		1	12	13	12 new SBOs, 1 Daimler CWA6
1955			4	4	4 SBOs
1956			5	5	2 AEC Regals, 3 Daimler CVD6
1957			2	12	5 AEC Regals, 7 Daimler CVD6
1958	25			25	20 Daimlers, 2 Guys, 3 AECs
1958		7		7	AEC B34F Contract Vehicles
1958				12	7 Daimler CVD6s, 5 AEC Regal coaches
1959			8	8	8 Bedford SB1s
1959	7	1		8	7 Daimler CWA6s, 1 Daimler C
1960			3	3	ex-Wakley, Axminster
1960		2	10	12	10 Bedford SB1s, 2 AEC Regal IV
1961		2			1 Daimler CVD6, 1 Maudsley M
1961			12	12	12 Bedford SBs ex-Feltham's
1961				6	6 Bedford SB1s
1961	15		6	21	6 Bedford SB1s, 11 AEC Regent IIIs, 4 Daimlers
1961		9		9	4 AEC Regal IIIs, 2Regal IVs 1 Crossley, 1 Maudslay Marathon 3
1962	9		6	15	6 Bedford SB5s, Daimler CVD6s
1962		5		5	3 AEC Regal IIIs, 2 Regal IV

Year				Total	
1963	16	5		21	16 Daimler CVD6s,1 Maudslay,
1964	18			18	17 AEC Regent IIIs, 1 Daimler CVD6
			7	7	Bedford SB5s
1965	3	3	7	13	Bedford SB5s x 7
1966			12	12	5 Bedford VAM 5 (Northern) 5 VAM 5(Hendon) 2 VAL 14s (H
1967		1	5	6	5 Bedford VAM70s, Bedford SB
1968			6	6	1 Bedford VAL(Northern) 5 Bedford VAM 70 (Hendon)
1969	12			12	10 Leyland PD2s, 2 AEC Regent IIIs
1970			5	5	1 Bedford VAL 70 (Northern) 2 VAM 70s(Northern) 2 VAM70s
1971	5		4	9	4 Bedford YRQs, 5 Leyland PD2s
1972			11	11	11 Bedford YRQs
1973			6	6	1 Bedford YRT, 5 YRQs.

Grand total: 435 vehicles, of which 123 were Bedford/Duple purchased new.

From the chart it will be noted that 110 double-deck vehicles were obtained solely for the purpose of site work (with one exception); 123 new Bedford coaches were purchased as well as three new Daimlers (all for the tours fleet), which leaves a total of 200 single-deck coaches some of which were used by the tours fleet and subsequently passed to the contract fleet. Some single-decked vehicles were purchased for contract use. The accompanying chart and the figures included have been compiled from company records and may differ from those published elsewhere.

CHAPTER 9

The Wessex Fleets

Although I am sure that purchases of vehicles would have been governed and authorised by the parent company, there are instances of vehicles going immediately into Wessex Motorways ownership. Many vehicles were also transferred from the main Bristol fleet to Chard. It is virtually impossible to track all movements so, for the purposes of this book; I have treated ALL vehicles as belonging to the main fleet and only entered them at the time of their purchase – disregarding later instances of transfers from Bristol to Chard and Chard to Bristol.

Wessex Coaches Ltd had acquired 75 vehicles at its formation and this made them the largest excursions and tours operator in Bristol - and possibly the South West. The familiar red and grey livery was derived from the colours of the two main constituent companies although I must say that it was more akin to Clifton Greys than Morning Star. All painting and repaints was done in house in the shed which could accommodate about 2-3 vehicles at a time in Wellington Street off Lawrence Hill. All vehicles were hand painted and the lettering to the boot doors and front and back glasses was applied by transfer and then varnished. The style of lettering was known as "hambone style". Every two years every vehicle had a complete repaint and in 1959, with the delivery of the DHY batch of Super Vegas, the fleet livery was reversed giving the coaches a grey roof with a larger area of red on the lower body. From 1959 onwards, with grey paint was tinted with green to give an entirely different appearance.

The vehicles taken over were of very mixed variety. Due to the war, many were not entirely satisfactory or suitable for the type of service that the new company intended for its patrons. A large programme of vehicle replacement and reconditioning was immediately embarked upon.

Fourteen Bedford OB/Duple Vistas were ordered and delivered in 1948/49, the two pre-war vehicles were completely rebuilt in Wessex workshops and

Two Austin K4/CXB models were delivered to Morning Star in 1947 immediately prior to the amalgamation. These coaches had 29-seat Plaxton bodywork, very similar to a Bedford OB. The regisration no. of the coach on the left would have been either KHW 19 or KHW 323. Both lasted until late 1954 with Wessex, and both eventually became mobile shops. The picture on the right, KHW 323, may be the same vehicle but it is shown as having been in service with Snell, Colerne by late 1954. After further disposal by Snell it became a mobile shop. (Author's Collection)

Bedford KHU 129 which originated with Morning Star.

BDV 11. A 1936 Leyland, ex-Devon General requisitioned by the Army in 1940 and re-bodied by Duple for Morning Star in 1946.

LAE 622, one of the first replacement vehicles, delivered new in 1948.

EPR 522 was an AEC Regal III with Gurney Nutting 37-seat bodywork. Originating with Clapcott Southampton, the vehicle came in in 1963 and lasted four years.

BV 1739 was an ex-Greys vehicle. New in 1932, it originally carried a Harrington body, being rebodied by Duple in 1946. In this guise it lasted with the group until 1959 and was then sold to a contractor for further use. There were two vehicles purchased at the same time and dealt with similarly. The sister vehicle was BV 2759, and it is seen parked behind.

This picture of TF 6616 shows it with the 1949 Lee Motor Bodies bodywork. The vehicle is shown two years earlier with its previous body in the earlier Morning Star group picture.

Charming early 1950s picture of BBV 418 collecting passengers in Crewkerne.

WH 5759 disgorging passengers in Axminster.

many others extensively overhauled. Some vehicles had received new bodies immediately prior to the war and others, mainly those that had suffered badly during the period of requisition by the Ministry immediately after. In 1952 six petrol engined Bedford SB/Duple Vegas were delivered and following the numerous Bedford OB/Duple Vistas these were to be the first of some 45 vehicles of Bedford/Duple Vega combination to be purchased new over the next 11 years.

By about 1955/6 Wessex had embarked upon a contract to convey the workers to and from the Berkeley Power Station construction site and in so doing probably set the parameters for two separate, but not entirely unconnected fleets. I will deal firstly with the Contract Fleet – the requirements of which lasted until the mid-1970s and the ultimate end of the company.

CHAPTER 9A

The Contract Fleet

This division was the anonymous face of Wessex Coaches Ltd. I am sure that there are readers who will be surprised to learn of its existence. No contract vehicles were painted in Wessex red and grey, all were painted blue and usually bore the name TAYLOR WOODROW in large letters on the lower panels of each side. The majority of the fleet were double-deckers of Daimler or AEC makes, and were always the cast-offs of Corporation and Municipal fleets. Added to these were the older vehicles of the main fleet that saw out their last days as contract vehicles, with the exception of the fleet vehicles transferred after 1973-4, all were driven until they became uneconomical to repair or to put new certificates on – they were then scrapped. The later vehicles were sold for further service at the end of the contracts. As will be seen from the pages of the PSV Fleet History PH4, the intake of second-hand vehicles was quite hectic during the period 1957-65.

There were various reasons for this, but Wessex was initially the main contractor for the carriage of labour from Bristol, Gloucester, Cheltenham, Dursley, and Tetbury and surrounds to the site of Berkeley Power Station. Construction at Berkeley started in 1955, and from that time on an extensive contract fleet was established to operate alongside the coaching fleet. For whatever reason, the Berkeley contract was terminated mid-stage and handed over to Mountain Transport Ltd of Chelsea, London. This latter company, I seem to recall, operated a number of ex-Red & White Guys and Albions from a base that they established in the Gloucestershire town of Berkeley. Wessex had initially operated several coaches a day on this contract. Regular drivers were used, and these drivers used their own vehicles, I dread to think of the man-hours that must have been spent in cleaning the interiors daily. I was told that during the winter most or all drivers stayed at Berkeley through the day and spent considerable time in the cinema at nearby Dursley. In the summer, however, older coaches, probably used solely on this contract, were left at the site and the drivers returned to Bristol in one vehicle to carry out other duties. Berkeley was the first of the power stations to be built on the banks of the River Severn, and was followed by Hinkley A – B and Oldbury (Wessex were not involved with Oldbury). I am further told that, at the peak, Mountain Transport had fifteen to twenty vehicles running into Bristol alone, and that these were parked in the old Cattle Market yard behind Temple Meads station. This, I think, illustrates the total number that Wessex would have been committed to had they retained the contract.

The Hinkley Power Station contract commenced in 1958 (overlapping Berkeley), with Taylor Woodrow Construction Group being the main contractor. Tenders were successfully submitted for the supply of vehicles. One can only surmise that the advent and success of this contract had caused Wessex to hand the Berkeley business to Mountain Transport, as, together with the extensive core business of tours and excursions in Bristol, the company would have been stretched to cope with such a volume of work. The Hinkley contract must have fitted the pattern of Wessex operations very much more easily. A large yard and ready-formed facility was available at Chard, where labour was readily available and cheap – and so, the Berkeley contract was passed over to Mountain Transport of Chelsea, London. Large numbers of the site workers came from the Chard/Bridgwater area to Hinkley Point, so what was more convenient? Drivers were recruited from those who already had jobs on the site. Selected workers were put through their driving test by the company to obtain licences, and were allowed to take their vehicles home with them at night. Thus we have the scenario of a driver collecting labourers on the way to the site in the morning, working all day on the site and then driving the personnel back home at night, parking his bus near to his home. Chard is not a million miles from the site and, whilst most buses were out-based at drivers' homes, they could easily be brought back to Chard for major repairs. Company fitters carried out minor repairs and servicing on site. What could have been better? Everyone was happy with the arrangement.

For this work, older second-hand heavyweight coaches were downgraded to site work and others bought in. The mortality rate of vehicles was very high; some drivers looked after their allotted vehicles, but others never even bothered to sweep theirs out. Second-hand deckers came into the fleet in ever-increasing numbers. The first appeared in 1954, and seems to have been HWB 491, an ex-Sheffield Corporation Daimler CWA6 of 1945 vintage – almost new – with a Duple wartime body. However, this was obtained to service the stage-carriage services operated by Chard & District, so this particular vehicle was not a contract vehicle – or directly owned by the parent company (see Chard & District section). Ernie Andrews was most likely responsible for the acquisition of the vehicles at this time, and that is probably why a large number of Daimlers featured in the purchases.

In 1958 Daimler D/Ds came from Coventry, EYMS Sunderland Corporation and Leeds, with three AECs from Newcastle Corporation as well as seven-single deck AEC Regal buses and seven Daimler coaches from various sources. These were obviously destined for Hinkley Point. When they were new and front line tour/service buses Daimlers must have been great, but with the contract vehicles in particular – we are talking of coaches and double-deckers that were up to fifteen years old, and not exactly from 'one careful driver' – these were a very different story. It was for this reason that (old) Daimlers, be they coaches or buses, were not the most popular vehicles in the fleet – certainly not with the Bristol drivers anyway. Most of the Daimlers that Wessex operated, were Daimler CVD6 and Daimler-engined, although there were three Gardner-powered motors and several with AEC units. Because of wartime problems and the bombing of the Radford Works in Coventry in May 1940, Daimler chassis production was curtailed and transferred to temporary premises in Wolverhampton. Daimlers were initially able to build chassis using stock parts until they ran out of engines.

At this point they turned to Gardners, and exactly 100 units were built using the 5LW engine combined with fluid flywheel transmission and flexible engine mounts to give a pleasant ride. Designated the CWG, mechanically these would have been very similar to the last buses supplied to Coventry before the war. Only three such vehicles entered the Wessex fleet, one from EYMS Hull, one from Coventry and one from Sunderland – all in 1958. Full Daimler chassis production resumed at Coventry in September 1943, but engines, with limited exceptions, now came from AEC, and a further 800 CWA6 were built up to the end of 1945, with more entering service in 1946-7. Some Gardner-engined vehicles were built for export. The CWA6 featured the AEC 7.7L engine, devoid of flexible engine mountings. Cast iron mountings were bolted direct to the chassis, a method that Bristols Ks used also. Add to this the lack of soft furnishings in the saloon, and I am told that the vehicle gave a very hard and noisy ride. These buses were, however, quite lively in performance if the engines were set to full power and not cut back to conserve precious fuel. See Geoffrey Hilditch's excellent book, *A Further Look at Buses*, for further information of this fascinating marque. Of the eighteen Wessex Daimlers which originated with Leeds City Transport, seventeen were CWA6s and only one was a CVD6. The Leeds vehicles had been constructed with utility bodies by Brush, Duple or Park Royal, but at least five had been re-bodied using second-hand Roe bodies of 1934-5 vintage, and looked rather archaic. In the pictures below, I show such a bus, and another accompanying two buses with wartime bodies, one Brush and one Park Royal. Although both would have been to otherwise identical specification, the bus on the right has the 1934 Roe body on a 1945 chassis. All of the later Leicester Daimlers were CVD6s. I should explain that the 'V' in CVD stood for Victory.

As I have said, the contract fleet was expanded to cope with the later extensive power station contracts taking in Berkeley (Glos.), Hinckley A & B, (Somerset), Wylfa (Anglesey), Sizewell and later, Sizewell B (Suffolk), Heysham (Lancs.), and Seal Sands (Hartlepool, County Durham).

Because of the urgency of need, second-hand buses were obtained from several sources – and some of them were shot before we even got them. I remember DDW127 coming from Newport Corporation. This Daimler CVD6 with a Brush H30/26R body was purchased as a scrapper for spares only, and was brought to Bristol on suspended tow. Somewhere on the journey, it had collided with a lorry load of hay and the offside windows were smashed and the panels ripped out, and it looked a very sorry mess when it arrived at Kingswood. However, such was the need that this bus was overhauled, rebuilt to a high standard in the company's own workshops, and sent to work at Sizewell where it lasted for another three years (see accompanying photograph).

Double-deckers operating these contracts were being driven through leafy lanes on the approaches to the site where they were never meant to go. Windows

DDW 127 a rebuilt ex-Newport Corporation Daimler GVD6/BRUSH

GUP 540 AEC Regal,
ex-Sunderland District,
Strachan body at Chard.

1944 chassis with 1934
Roe bodyork.

Two wartime AEC-
engined Daimlers
and one with 1935
bodywork. All vehicles
shown on this page are
ex-Leeds Corporation.

were invariably smashed, top panels were stoved in and, bearing in mind that these buses had already supposedly ended their service life with a local authority, the mechanical components took a bashing as well. Thus several vehicles were cannibalised. As the Hinkley A contract was running down, the Sizewell, one came on stream (1961), and this was overlapped with the one at Wylfa (1963), to be followed in later years by Sizewell B, Heysham and Hartlepool. Bill Jones would have taken responsibility for the purchasing following Ernie Andrews sudden death, but it is significant that he did not purchase one single Leyland during this period. It was not until after his retirement that ten Leyland PD2s came into the fleet from Great Yarmouth. This is surprising considering Bill's background at Morning Star, where the 'favourite' make of vehicle was Leyland. Wessex had bought the three new Daimlers back in the late '40s, through the influence of L.W. and Ernie Andrews, although these might be said to have been inherited. From 1959-63 forty-four Daimlers were purchased from Leicester Corporation (all CVD6s). AEC were the next most popular, twenty-five Regents came from Leicester and others from South Wales. I personally found these latter AEC examples to be very good buses, and they were fitted with the air-assisted transmission and air brakes as standard. Leicester buses had bodywork by Willowbrook and Roberts (both local Midlands builders) and Brush.

Anyone familiar with the Daimler transmissions will no doubt have a story to tell about the fluid flywheel and pre-selector 'gearbox'. AEC also produced a pre-selector box, as in the London RT/RMs, but Daimler did not use air assistance as AEC did in those days. The drive bands within the 'gearbox' were operated and changed mechanically by the very heavy movement of the gear change pedal, as one would use a clutch. One waited at, say, the traffic lights, and while waiting applied the handbrake, engaging first gear by way of the heavy cast quadrant lever on the steering column. Then one pressed the left-hand pedal to engage the gear – the lights went green – off with the handbrake, a little throttle and off we go. Fine, we are rolling. As soon as one moved, one selected second gear, which would not engage until one pressed the 'clutch' pedal. One did this and, sometimes, – BANG – that solid cast iron lump of a foot pedal came eighteen inches out of the floor at the speed of a space rocket on its way to Mars, and trapped the driver's left leg under the seat frame, that is, if his leg was still in rigid form and not floating about below the knee.

This was a common fault with all Daimlers, not just these ones. Bill Jones had warned me about the gear change bands when I first drove a Daimler. Luckily I was never caught. Some vehicles were worse than others. The way that the problem could (hopefully) be avoided was just by keeping the inside of the ball of the left foot on the left-hand edge of the pedal, pressing and holding the pedal down for a count of three. If it did fly back, and one was unlucky, the worst that would happen was that it might graze one's ankle, but one would soon have learnt to be quick enough to have slid one's foot off sideways in time – and never to attempt a 'racing change' again. To return it to the norm one had to lean back in the seat, both feet on the pedal and, with a great deal of effort, push it back in against the spring. There are still one or two in preservation – if you see one, just ask the driver and he will bear out my stories. Now, the AECs were always my personal favourite. The pre-selector pedal had about three inches of travel, was air assisted and the easiest thing in the world to operate, the same as a London RT and, added to that, it had a nice comfortable rubber pedal cover. I must tell you a little story at this stage.

I took my 'PSV' test in March 1962. It was agreed that I take an 'all types' test, and that whatever double-decker was in the yard at the time would the one that I would use. The day came, and the only vehicle present was JUO 566, an AEC Regent III with Weymann H30/26R body, identical to a London RT (except in the body). This vehicle was ex-Western Welsh, but originally Devon General, and a pleasure to drive. It was fitted with a pre-selector gearbox, and having taken and passed my test on this vehicle my licence would be stamped 'Pneumocyclic gearbox only', the same as for a London Transport driver who had his test on a similar vehicle. George Bascombe, the foreman fitter, presented every new driver for his test and we duly met the examiner. This examiner, who I will not name, was a friend of George and regularly tested our prospective drivers. George said to me, 'Whatever you do, don't mention the gearbox'. Formalities over, I was given a route and told where I was required to do the reversing test. Off we went. One hour later I was back in Anchor Road. I knew that I had botched up one part of the reversing section. I stood on the platform, the examiner sat one side of the lower deck and George sat the other. They carried on talking and completely ignored me for at least five minutes until Mr Examiner looked up and said, "you doing anything tonight? You need some reversing tuition!' Now up to a couple of months previous I had been driving the largest rigid van in Bristol, as well as articulated vehicles for six years prior to that, and knew that I should have done better. I could reverse that Luton van built on a Bedford SBO coach chassis through the eye of a needle if necessary, so I asked if I could have another go to prove that I could do it. Mr Examiner said, 'No, you have passed, and I must congratulate you on your gear changing. I never felt one'. I am positive that he winked when he said it. My licence was never stamped, had it been it would have meant that I was not licensed to drive a coach/bus with a conventional 'stick' gearbox. Thank goodness that I never had to do this in a Daimler.

There was a period when several Leicester Daimlers were stored in Kingswood garage for a considerable time awaiting new contracts, and I can vouch for the faults with these beasts. If they were taxed we used them on various jobs, and sometimes on Saturday football trips to the Bristol Rovers or City grounds. Bristol Grammar School to Failand sports ground – boy did they boil climbing Failand Hill on the Clevedon road with a full load plus all the sports equipment! – and this was a regular job throughout the school year. I recall an occasion when I covered a return Weston advertised day-trip one summer's evening with a double-decker – we must have been really pushed for vehicles that day. Up to three buses a day were used to take workers from Bristol to various parts of the M4, when that was under construction, between what is now J19 to 18. Another two deckers a day were used to carry GPO personnel from central Bristol to what was then the secret underground city at Corsham – and another was based out at Timsbury for this purpose. In 1963 Bath hosted a military tattoo. Troops and personnel were housed all over Wiltshire at various army bases and, for the four to five day period, I suppose there must have been at least thirty-odd vehicles required in total. The contract belonged to Bleakens Coaches of Hawkesbury Upton, but it was in the height of the busy season and spare vehicles were hard to find. Ted Bleaken brought coaches in from everywhere, and we had a very good slice of those numbers. A few of our double-deckers were used and, as it transpired, this was a piece of luck, because the mascot of the Welsh Guards was a very large Billy goat and he travelled reasonably happily on the platform of one of these buses.

Most Leicester Daimlers and AECs were despatched directly to the sites at Sizewell or Wylfa, as I remember; this was only logical, of course, Leicester being half way to either destination. Until I found the accompanying photos to prove the point, I was not even aware that the company ran single-deckers such as the Sunderland AECs in contract blue. Any buses that we had long term at Kingswood always seemed to be of Leicester origin, probably because Sizewell A was running down and they were not wanted in North Wales. As I have said, the Daimlers generally were not at all liked and certainly not compatible with the terrain of Anglesey.

During my time with the company, it would mainly have been the Kingswood or Chard drivers that encountered the contract buses. Clifton drivers would have considered it very demeaning if they were asked to drive one, although they were no doubt very pleased with the winter overtime when vehicles needed to be collected or ferried between sites. Most of them were painted all over blue and lettered for Taylor Woodrow; others were known to have finished their working lives in the colours of their previous operator(s). The majority of the buses came from Leicester Corporation, and the next volume supplier was Leeds, but others came from a variety of sources – Coventry, Sunderland District, Newcastle Corp., Western Welsh. Later – lo and behold! – the first Leylands came from Great Yarmouth in 1969 with a batch of ten, followed in 1972 with

FBC 674 in service at
Leicester.

FBC 674 working at
Sizewell.

GR 9098 speeding
through Bridgwater *c.*
1959.

GUP 538 at Chard *c.* 1959.

FBC 308, an ex-Leicester AEC Regent III with Brush body at Wylfa.

The lone 1949 Crossley with Yeates bodywork.

Two very tidy Regents in North Wales, FBC 299 & 308, both ex-Leicester.

FBC 670, a Daimler CVD6 at Sizewell, also ex-Leicester.

Leicester City Transport FBC 541 in the condition in which we used the vehicle for some time, still in Leicester's colours. It is seen here parked outside of St George Library and opposite Cliff Cornford's coffee shop. Cliff often did afternoon school jobs for us at Kingswood. As far as I recall this vehicle and a couple of others never worked on a construction site other than locally on the M4 and Littleton-on-Severn contracts. (Authors collection)

FBC 541 approaching Bristol Bus Station on a Saturday afternoon, probably from either the Littleton-on-Severn contract or M4 construction site for McAlpine's. I am driving this one. Daimler CVD6 with a Roberts's body. (Author's collection/C. Routh)

FBC 311 in North Wales

EKV 957. The ex-Coventry Guy Arab.

another five. Other single purchases came from other sources, probably through dealers, as indeed some of the aforementioned would have done. Bear in mind that, certainly during the early '60s, Bill Jones or Ernie Andrews was paying little money for a vehicle, but they earned good money in Wessex employ.

As time progressed, even as late as 1962 when I joined, the two fleets became further and further apart. Graham Cottey, who had joined as a driver at Chard, was placed in charge of the contract operation by 1963. He was responsible for the day-to-day organisation and operation of the fleet while Hinkley Point was still in progress. I think that he did his best, but at that time was provided with some very rough vehicles, as can be imagined by the numbers shown in the records to be 'scrapped at Chard'. He persevered to improve the quality of what he had to work with, and it can be seen from the photo's that the condition of the early Daimlers at Hinkley and Sizewell bears no relationship to the later AECs etc. at Wylfa. In 1958 batches of deckers were purchased for Hinkley, and they lasted four years at maximum. The first batch of Leeds deckers was purchased in 1958. Some of these were withdrawn and scrapped in 1962, having spent their time on the Hinkley Point contract, but some had not been licensed for use until 1960-61, so they did not have too long a working life with Wessex. Having said that, others of the batch did last for a little longer – in two cases until 1965.

By 1965 Graham had greatly improved the appearances and maintenance standards of the vehicles, and not only from a practical side. Graham also instilled some discipline into the drivers, who were still employed on a part-time basis. He soon got rid of the ones who misused and abused their vehicles. As the records show, scrapping took place at Chard and on site, but some buses came back through Kingswood and were collected by a local character called 'Cash' Davies who lived in a caravan at Oldland Common. Some buses (and coaches) were broken up in a field near to his 'base', and some were taken to a disused quarry at Clutton in North Somerset to be disposed of. 'Cash' would salvage any good parts and try to sell them back to Bill Jones.

As said, the Daimlers were OK for the operating conditions in Hinkley and Suffolk, each with (near) flat terrain, but were soon found to be very unsuitable for Anglesey. Therefore a number of AECs came in, from Leicester and South Wales. These buses were more durable to the conditions, and I remember that the ones that I met were very good vehicles. Daimlers, and later AEC Regent IIIs, came in profusion from 1961 onwards from Leicester, and were despatched to Sizewell (Daimlers) or Wylfa (AECs) directly. The bodywork on these was both by Roberts and Willowbrook and, from my memory they were in good condition when they arrived and lasted well. Surplus Daimlers were parked at Kingswood depot, but I do not recall many AECs being there for long. FBC 541 and 666 (Daimlers) amongst others spent their entire time parked there. I don't think either bus ever went away on site work, but were used as and when necessary at Kingswood, and were in fact each broken up by 'Cash' in early 1967. Sizewell had finished by that time and Daimlers were not much use anywhere else, in any case by this time their 'tickets' had expired.

There were also the motorway construction and many other local contracts for which the vehicles were used. I recall that at least three were used permanently each day for McAlpine's on the stretch of the M4 from J19 to 18 – a rather steep climb for the old girls over an unmade road surface. This stretch has recently been modified to include a fourth 'climbing' lane, found necessary even with the massive power outputs available in modern machines. The driver had to carry five gallons of water with him because a Leicester Daimler would be boiling by the time it got to Tormarton. If the bell was rung to stop at Lyde Green (just off the Westerleigh Road now) – it was as much as the fully loaded bus could do to pull away on the incline and make it to the Tormarton A46 Bridge. Drivers were forced to slow to a speed where everyone could jump off without stopping the vehicle. The roads in Leicester are near flat, and this bus was designed for that City. One driver ignored the request to stop at the bottom one morning and so held his speed up the hill. I think that it was a part-timer involved, but I know that we could never put him on that duty again because one Irish labourer was made late for work and threatened to kill him.

As I have said, most of the second-hand purchases were collected directly from the previous owner, usually in the winter when company drivers were available, and driven directly to the site. We never saw them in Bristol. Occasionally, some would park overnight at Kingswood if a site driver was to come down and collect a vehicle that we had stored or had maybe been sent up from Chard. At one time, we had about twelve vehicles parked in our garage, but the norm would be a maximum of one or two. Along the inner right-hand wall of the 'back' garage at Kingswood was an open pit running the full length of the garage, and someone reversed into this one day with a D/D – no, it was not me. We invariably used to keep this pit covered with parked vehicles to avoid any accidents, but I am afraid that these did happen. During the peak weeks the stored buses (if taxed) would be used to carry out school's and workers' contract work, even the odd private hire, and at weekends (even the out-based) could be fully utilised on University or Bristol Grammar School work. I remember two deckers once being hired by a film company. They were repainted pink, if I remember rightly, and had to drive around in a circle in front of The Mansion House on Clifton Downs with the sequence speeded up to make it look as if they were doing about 80mph – a Daimler doing 80mph?!

I mentioned earlier that Daimlers had a problem with the gear changes, but in the case of the ex-Leicester buses there was an even greater problem – the brakes. Now, I was never meant to fully understand the workings of the braking system on these buses, but it transpired that no one else did either. A leather bag, pressurised to some almighty pressure with nitrogen, was inside a cylinder full of brake fluid, also pressurised. I believe that it was known as a Lockheed Hydrovac System. If the leather bag perforated or, even worse, burst, all pressure was lost and no brakes were operative. The system was a nightmare. Bill Liddington, our Kingswood fitter, and I went to the Commercial Motor Show in London around 1964 and Bill said that he wanted to get to the bottom of this system. We went onto the Lockheed stand and spoke to various gentlemen in their posh suits and no one knew what we were talking about, until a chap came out of the little office and said, 'I know, ex-Leicester Corporation'. He went on to tell us that this system had been condemned by the manufacturers before it was even specified by Leicester. As far as they were concerned, they could not help us and did not really want to know.

I was descending Gloucester Road, Bristol, (a busy shopping area) one summer Saturday afternoon, returning from one of the construction sites with one of these machines. I pressed the pedal and nothing happened. To cut a long story short, I changed the shape of a couple of cars that day. When I looked back into the lower saloon to get someone to witness the fact that the pressure gauge was reading empty everyone had scarpered, my load of 'paddies' had vanished, and my bag had literally burst. I rang Les Jay, the foreman fitter and he said 'Oh yes. Don't worry about it, bring it back on the 'gearbox', but I refused, and he came out to fetch it himself. One of the Daimlers (FBC 676) was decapitated by a low bridge in Suffolk somewhere, but the fitters at Sizewell made a very tidy job of converting it to a tree lopper. It was later brought back to Kingswood and used as a mobile workshop and this considerably prolonged its active life, as it lasted far longer than the rest of the batch. At that time, we had a young second fitter at Kingswood, Les Hancock. On Friday nights in September and October when the Blackpool Lights tours were on, he would drive up to Lancashire, park up where he could be contacted and attend to any breakdowns or emergencies immediately. I cannot remember him ever being used, but he enjoyed the ride.

During the early '70s many of the older coaches were transferred to the Power Station contract sites. These were returned from Chard, to where they had been moved in 1965/70. Ownership was transferred back to the main fleet, and these ex-Feltham's vehicles and the 1955 batch of four 38-seaters were on the move again, firstly to Hartlepool and later to Heysham to operate within the contract fleet. These were followed by most of the DHY batch of Super Vegas, and also, strangely enough, all of the second-hand acquisitions – 821 CUP, 157 ALH, THR 240 and 6469 NU. Pictures show that they were well maintained and kept very spruce. Some were eventually painted a very pale green colour. Whether this was

Also in use at Heysham are UAE 963 and 965, now relegated to contract use and seen together with AEX 331, one of the ex-Great Yarmouth PD2s.

Also relegated was ex-Felthams UND 714, shown here in the company of EX 9073, an ex-Great Yarmouth Corporation Leyland PD2. The standards had most certainly improved by *c.* 1970 when this photo was taken. They even had route numbers at this time.

The rural air of North Wales.

Above and below: 972 and 973 shown after relegation to contract duties, probably at Heysham after being transferred to Chard ownership in 1969. 972 was withdrawn and sold in 1972. A year later 973 rejoined the Bristol fleet for continued use.

prior to the sale of the vehicles or whether they were painted into the light, plain colours, similar to that used by the ex-Great Yarmouth and Colchester Leyland double-deckers during their lives as Wessex contract buses, is not known. At the end of the later contract, Heysham, some vehicles were broken up on site and locally, but several others were sold for further PSV use. This alone speaks volumes for the lifetime maintenance standards of the Wessex fleet.

At the end of the Heysham contract, the remaining serviceable coaches were painted white and sold to operators for further PSV use

CHAPTER 9B

The Tours Fleet

Although I am sure that second-hand purchases of vehicles would have been governed and authorised by the parent company, there are instances of vehicles going immediately into Chard ownership. Many vehicles were also transferred from the main Bristol fleet to Chard – and back again. It is virtually impossible to track all movements so, for the purposes of this book, I have treated all vehicles as belonging to the main fleet, and only entered them at the time of their purchase – disregarding later instances of transfers from Bristol to Chard and Chard to Bristol.

As has been noted, seventy-five serviceable vehicles made up the core of the fleet in 1948 at the formation. Apart from three new Daimler CVD6s, two Duple-bodied, and one by Plaxton delivered in 1948-9, all orders placed for new vehicles throughout the history of the company were for Bedford chassis carrying Duple bodies. Orders were not placed every year – there are notable gaps. Obviously, financial constrictions played their part, and although the decision to buy vehicles would have been a board decision, the man who held the purse strings was the very astute company secretary, Mr Bellamy (more about him later). I am sure that he was not a man to let the company go into debt.

Of the 1948 arrivals, three were new Bedford OBs with Duple C29F bodies to the usual style, but there was also one other OB (LHT 971) delivered in this year, and this one is listed as 'chassis was a reconstruction by Lee Motors of Bournemouth'. No more is known about this one. Could it have been a OWB or pre-war chassis WTB rebuild? Also purchased new was one of the Daimler CVD6/Plaxton C33F. The only other vehicle listed as 'new' was one of the two Wessex rebuilds, an Albion PV70, LAE 61, the chassis of which left the factory of its Scottish manufacturer in 1932. The C28F bodywork of this vehicle was rebuilt on the framework of the original in Wessex workshops. In 1948, such a vehicle was given a brand new registration within the current issuing sequence. Nothing is known of previous owners.

In 1949, no less than twelve new Bedford OBs joined the fleet, together with the two aforementioned Daimlers, which I again believe to have been previously ordered by Clifton Greys. The only other delivery this year was the other rebuild, again with a new registration, LHY 431. This vehicle, mentioned and pictured elsewhere, was also rebuilt by Wessex themselves and was based on a 1936 AEC Regal chassis, and was previously operated by Rover of Aberdeen. The vehicle was purchased directly from the War Department and powered by a 7.7L AEC oil engine, but only lasted with Wessex until 1952. Three further OBs were delivered in 1950, making a total of nineteen of that marque. These were all petrol-engined, with conventional (at that time) Lockheed hydraulic two-line braking system with no servo assistance. I was employed as an apprentice fitter in the '50s at Cathedral Garage in Bristol, and several of these coaches came to us in, I believe, the winter of 1952/3 to be converted to diesel power. Perkins P6 engines were fitted – and, boy, did they rattle! – on tick-over the whole coach shook. While the engine conversions were taking place, the braking systems were modified and up-rated. Heavy duty Clayton Dewandre servo units were added to the braking system. This servo increased the braking pressure by two-and-a-half times, and I remember being delighted to be involved in that part of the conversions. Welch's (the Bedford agent), Coventry, and Jeff's (Perkins agent) and Bristol Motor Company (Morris Commercial) each shared this work with Cathedral Garage.

Next to arrive were the six SBs in 1952, again with petrol engines. I believe that Wessex converted these in their own workshop, but again fitted Perkins P6 engines by 1956. I had finished my apprenticeship and left Cathedral by then, but heard that these later SBs shook even more than the OBs after conversion. They each lasted only six years in Wessex ownership. Each was sold out directly in 1958, without even being transferred to Chard. Having said that, the records do state that all were used for further PSV service, and I recall seeing OHY 398 still running around the Oxford area with Percivals in the late '60s. According to PSV Circle records, it was not withdrawn until mid-1971, when it would have been nineteen years old. At least two of the six eventually finished up in Cyprus, being exported in 1959, and I would imagine that each had undergone extensive rebuilds during the intervening years, probably lasting until the '80s at least ...

In 1954 came what were always referred to as 'the SAEs': SAE 951 to SAE 962. This was the start of the registration number sequence, which lasted from then until the last new vehicle purchases were made in 1973-4. All registration numbers followed on numerically, making the duty rosters easier, as drivers' names were put against the numerical listing. The numbers reached 995 (OHW) in 1962, and the next deliveries in 1964 commenced at 950 (WAE) and went backwards ultimately reaching LAE 895L with the final delivery in 1973. In practice, only 996 to 999 were missing.

Collecting the 1952 SBs from Hendon when new; this appears to be Les Jay driving the first one with a further two following.

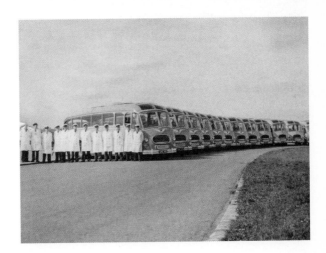

Twelve 'SAEs' from the 1954 delivery, posed at the Sea Walls on Durdham Down, Bristol.

Manufacturer's picture of 1952 showing the very tidy lines of the original 37-seat Vega body constructed by Duple for the Bedford SB.

This fine period picture shows a Bedford OB, LHU 948, collecting passengers outside of the Whiteladies Road Head Office for an afternoon tour on a sunny day in June 1949. Note the sunshine roof of the vehicle, the handwritten advertising and the driver's regulation uniform. The latter two items did not change for the life of Wessex – the sunshine roof did. The vehicle following appears to be LHT 971, the Lee-bodied OB. I was intrigued by this picture because the departure time from this point was 2.15pm, and yet the clock shows 2.32pm.

Alec Lusher and his family lived in a flat above the offices in 1949 and Alec's son Geoff has given me the answer. The clock mechanism was faulty for a considerable period, and being rather unusual was rather expensive to repair. It was consequently left in this condition at the time Geoff lived there. I had never noticed this before but if you look at the ring of numbers you will note that it contains both Roman and Arabic numerals – also an unusual feature.

Manufacturer's Picture 1954, fitted with the notorious Perkins R6 engine.

SAE 962. The highest numerical of the batch, pictured outside of The First Inn in England, St Just, while on the Cornish Extended Tour.

UAE 965 in the 'as delivered' paint scheme, with a red roof.

UAE 966, as delivered.

SAE 959, as delivered.

As repainted 1960, UAE 965.

SAE 961 at Victoria in the new colours. Note also the later treatment of the bottom mouldings. This was another unique intricacy of Wessex design after the repaints.

PHR 791 (ex-Felthams) at Dunster, August 1963.

A period advert from Duple Motor Bodies Ltd.

The twelve 38-seater Duple-bodied SBOs of the 1954 delivery, together with a further four in 1956, were probably the most notorious vehicles ever owned by any coach operator. Most operators had problems with the (then) new Perkins R6 5.56L engine, but no one to my knowledge had the problems that Wessex suffered. I was told by the fitting staff during my time with the company that very many replacement engines were fitted to the sixteen vehicles (including the UAEs of 1955). I was given to understand that Perkins fitted these engines under warranty in a space of eighteen months. The situation came to such a pitch that, wherever in the country a coach broke down, Perkins Diesels themselves would be informed, and they would recover it back to Peterborough or elsewhere, fit another engine and return the coach to Bristol. Another company that took this model in any significant number was George Ewer – Grey Green, but I know that they specified Leyland engines rather than Perkins units. Eastern National took a further eighteen and specified Gardner 4LK engines – I wonder how much smoke they put out?

The main problems were to do with the rear engine crankshaft oil-seals blowing out, and also the timing chains were liable to stretch, leading to smashed timing-chain covers. I have already said that I drove a van built on the same 1955 SBO chassis with a Perkins R6, and that blew out only one back seal in 208,000 miles, and let me down only twice in six years. I put this down to the fact that I did my own regular servicing. The timing chain was renewed about four times, as I recall, and I changed the engine oil and filters every 4,000 miles, only ever using Shell Rotella oil. Besides, the vehicle only had one driver from the time that it was eight months old with about 25K on the clock.

The 1955 SBO/R6 that I drove for almost six years from the day that I was twenty-one years old.

Another problem with the SAEs was this. Immediately after the first engine change, and the disturbance of the driveline, the centre prop-shaft bearings started giving problems. Bill Jones was a real old-fashioned fleet engineer. He had the answer to any problem. He had the centre-bearing casing drilled and tapped as if to take a grease nipple. He soldered a cocoa tin to a piece of copper pipe, threaded the end of the pipe and screwed it into the centre bearing. This was done to the entire batch. Every morning the driver had to check his engine oil *and* lift up the centre inspection flap halfway down the aisle and top this tin up with gear oil – problem solved – but I bet it made a mess of the garage floor. When the new Bedford 300 series engine became available from 1959 onwards, it was fitted to the whole batch and no more problems occurred. At the end of their life, for all of these aforementioned problems, these vehicles must have paid for themselves over and over again. In my day they were probably the hardest-worked vehicles of the fleet: they were used for contract work, tours, private hire or express work seven days a week, and were generally very tidy motors.

In appreciation of their good service, SAE 951-955 and 961 lasted until 1967, while SAE 956-960 and also 962 lasted with Wessex until 1969. All were sold to Arlington's, the dealers who supplied the new Bedford's to the company, and they were sold on again for further PSV use.

A couple of little known facts concerning the delivery of the SAEs concern the design of the moquette used on the interior upholstery. All new vehicles delivered from this delivery onward, from 1954 to 1973, used a design of cloth which was unique to Wessex. I found seats covered in this material in one of the two OBs preserved by Tours (Isle of Man) Ltd, and was immediately able to identify them as from a Wessex vehicle. No other operator could use this material. The batch of registration numbers first issued to these vehicles were prefixed SHT. Alec Lusher said that there was no way that he would have coaches within the fleet with such numbers so the local licensing office changed the batch issue to SAE. As already mentioned these vehicle registrations started the numerical sequence continued up to the end. In 1955 four more 38-seater SBOs were purchased. I think that it must have been a very persuasive Perkins salesman who pulled that sale off. These were registered as UAE 963-966 and again fitted with the R6, replaced as mentioned above.

By 1960 Perkins engines had been removed from each of the sixteen 38-seaters, and new Bedford 300 engines were fitted. Bill Jones was involved with Bedford, in the design of this engine. For some reason, no further new vehicles were purchased between 1955 and 1959. I remember, as an outsider, thinking that Wessex was seriously slipping behind their competitors in vehicle standards as, in 1955, the wheelbase length of an SB was increased from 17ft 2in to 18ft to accommodate the 41-seater bodies. Wessex never purchased any of the original

Vega (butterfly front) 41-seat models, but I believe that these were only offered with petrol engines. Bedford and Wessex must have fallen out with Perkins by this time, and it was not until the intro of their own 300 engine that Bedford again offered the diesel alternative – the Bedford 'Super Vega'. For a period of four years Wessex only had 38-seater vehicles on their stock, when 41-seaters were available for hire elsewhere, albeit with petrol engines, and were being used by their competitors. As he was involved in the design I can now believe that Bill was awaiting the advent of the new 4.9ltr engine before purchasing any new vehicles.

In 1959 came the eight Super Vegas, 967-974 DHY. These were fitted with Bedford's own 300cc diesel engines, which were changed for the 330cc by 1963 – and were much better for it. With the 1959 delivery came the advent of the new paint scheme which was to become standard for all vehicles. In 1960 came the HHTs 975-984, still with the small engine, as Bedford's up-rated engine did not come out until 1962, and again changed to the 330 by 1963-4. 1961, same

YHY 370, ex-Felthams was the first coach that I used after gaining my licence. This was for a tour to Bourton-on-the-Water at Easter 1962, when it still had its original petrol engine and Feltham's colours. This picture shows it after relegation to contract duties at Seal Sands late in its life, but still in very good condition.

An ex-Feltham's vehicle that became rather an 'odd bod', being one of only two Plaxton-bodied vehicles in the main fleet in 1960s. This was Stan Peacock's coach from new in Feltham's time, and he kept it for a further three years with Wessex. It was always kept immaculate by Stan and still looks fairly good here, after it had passed to contract duties at Heysham in late 1967.

again, the LHUs came in, 985 - 990. These were good because this was the year that the single piece screen was introduced, and I think that it much improved the frontal appearance of the vehicle.

January 1961 saw the purchase of the Feltham's fleet (Kingswood Queen), of Moravian Road, Kingswood, Bristol.

Of the sixteen vehicles involved, four were sold immediately after the deal was done, so only twelve vehicles actually joined the fleet. Feltham's vehicles were always immaculate, in light blue with a cream relief. Of these twelve vehicles, ten carried Duple Vega (butterfly) bodies and two were Plaxtons – the only two Plaxton-bodied Bedford's in the front-line fleet. Eleven were 41-seaters, and one only was a 38-seater (RUE 696). All were Bedford petrol-engined and were new between 1956 and 1958. Feltham's policy was to buy mainly new vehicles, but there were four second-hand ones among these twelve. Now Mr. G.J. Jones had always said that he would never run a petrol-engined coach (for obvious reasons), and that if any driver bought a diesel car, he would sack him. So the petrol engines had to go. I think I am right in saying that five petrol engines survived into the 1962 season – I remember that I took YHY 370 to Bourton-on-the-Water on Easter Monday of that year, with a petrol engine, but it was changed immediately after and was converted before the 1962 season became busy. I believe 370 was the last to survive with a petrol engine. Until conversion, these petrol-engined vehicles had as little use as possible. In the place of the petrol units went second-hand Bedford 300 diesels, donated by newly purchased second-hand units.

Every ex-Feltham's vehicle retained its four-speed gearbox, which was not the perfect match to this power unit. Bill Jones would visit the local scrap yards seeing where he could buy second-hand engines/lorries. It was a standing joke that he would buy a scrap lorry, remove the engine and give it a 'Bill Jones Overhaul', before fitting it into a coach chassis. This consisted of a wash down with paraffin, being swilled off with a hosepipe before fitting. The rest of the useful bits would be robbed from the lorry and stored, whilst the remains went straight to the scrap yard. The converted vehicles were extremely noisy to both the driver and front seat passengers. Extensive sound deadening measures were taken with the converted vehicles: a specially made fibreglass bonnet and a considerable amount of foam insulation around the front bulkhead and beneath the dash was fitted, but they were still considerably noisier than a standard Duple fitment. In all fairness the two Plaxtons were far quieter, with a completely different sound to the Duples. Feltham's vehicles, not having worked as hard in their previous life, were very good to drive, although slightly underpowered due in part to the four-speed gearbox. While on the subject of replacement engines, I remember occasions in the height of the season when coaches came in at night with blown engines. Spare engines were kept but, if one was not available, Bill would be out looking next morning, would buy a second-hand engine, and that coach would be on afternoon tour at the very least that day. If an engine was in stock it would have been replaced overnight, and that coach made available for early morning tour if necessary.

It was at this time that Autolube Chassis Lubrication was being introduced to the fleet, and ex-Feltham's vehicles were the first to be treated. Coaches were sent to Coventry & Jeff's in Bristol to have this fitted. I must admit that this made the ride much more comfortable, but I also remember that as you turned a left or right corner you could feel the spring eye slide across the shackle pin, and, worse than that, we never had a clean garage floor again.

In '62 came 991-995 OHW Bedford Super Vegas, with the full screen *and* air brakes – the first in the fleet. These were also the first to be delivered with the new, larger Bedford 330 engines. The 41-seater Super Vegas were still built at Hendon, although Duple had taken over Burlingham in early 1960. The extra capacity at Blackpool was much needed by Duple, as they would have been restricted in the building of bodies on the longer chassis now becoming available, such as the VAL. Production of the VAL was transferred from Hendon to Blackpool and the Blackpool-designed 'Firefly' appeared in 1963.

Duple were going through a period of model changes over the next two years and no new coaches were purchased until the start of the 1964 season, when a break was made with tradition. Instead of buying Duple Hendon bodies, as previously, they went for the Duple Firefly, the first Duple model to come out of the Burlingham factory in Blackpool. This was known as a Duple Northern body, and was styled very much on the lines of its Burlingham predecessor, the Gannet. Seven of these were delivered. The numbers started to go backwards now. There had been a 951 with the SAEs, so these were numbered 950-944 WAE. The bodies on these coaches were entirely different to the Super Vegas of the past few years, and they looked good.

I always thought that this was a very under-rated body, not altogether popular with other operators by virtue of numbers sold. The body type was fitted to Fords and lightweight Albions as well as Bedfords. Seven more came along in 1965 (937-943), although five were delivered and registered in December 1964, and three (BHU 937/8/9C) were not registered until Easter 1965. I recall taking 937 on its very first tour on the afternoon of Easter Sunday 1965 when brand new. These were the last 41-seaters delivered. One of the features that I remember with this model is that, at last, Duple realised that the driver needed warmth as well as his passengers on a cold night. I recall returning from somewhere one winter's night driving an HHT and I had my overcoat on. Through the mirror, I could see passengers in their shirtsleeves and I was eventually asked to turn the heating down. This did not happen with a Firefly.

972 DHY appears to be advertising the company whilst parked near the War Memorial on Bristol City Centre. I wonder who vandalised the grille? This picture must have been taken in early 1959 when the vehicle was new.

978 HHT, looking new when collecting passengers from Whiteladies Road …

… and with the late Norman Sykes, my mentor.

992 heading into Bretonside Bus Station, Plymouth, no doubt on the Plymouth, Princetown & Two Bridges tour.

A Firefly from the first delivery

As a point of interest for those people unfamiliar with the types of engines used, the capacities were as follows.

Perkins P6	4.7l	Converted to and not fitted by Bedford
Perkins R6	5.562l	Bedford SBO and fitted by the manufacturer
Bedford 300	4.9l	Bedford SBI six-cylinder Diesel
Bedford 330	5.4l	Bedford SB5 & VAM 5 six-cylinder Diesel

The VAL 14 was fitted with a 6.17-litre Leyland 0.400 engine. The VAL 70 and VAM 70 were fitted with Bedford's own 7.6-litre engine. In 1968 the codes were changed by Bedford – but I will not confuse the issue.

In 1965 the maximum length was relaxed to 11m, and in came the 45-seaters. This was a mixed delivery, as five were Duple Viscounts (EAE 932-936C) from the Blackpool factory, and three Duple Viceroys from Hendon (JAE 929-931D). Why the split I do not know, unless it was due to a variance in availability dates. It will be noted from the registration numbers (which then changed each 1 January) that the five Viscounts were delivered in late 1965, and the three Viceroys in 1966. These were built on the VAM 5 chassis with the 330, 5.4l engine still mounted at the front, even though other manufacturers were putting their engines under floor. The drive was through a Clark gearbox built under licence by Turner. VAM stood for VA series of medium length. The VAL was the VA series of long length, to the maximum newly permitted 36 feet. Particularly the northern VAMs caused a few problems when new. Drivers found them difficult to keep in a straight line and did not like them, but the situation was somewhat remedied by moving the fuel tanks from the nearside of the chassis to the offside. EAE 932C suffered an early demise, and was written off after a serious accident in Southmead Road, Bristol, in 1971. Also delivered new this year were two Bedford VAL 14s. This was the six-wheeler, three-axle model with sixteen-inch wheels. JAE 927D and 928D were fitted with the Viceroy Bodies, 6.17L Leyland engines and power steering. Wessex was well behind the competition with these new and innovative machines. Western Roadways of Bristol by now had a sizeable number of the model after taking delivery of the first in 1963.

Bill Jones had his doubts about the design, and told me at the time that he wanted other operators to sort out the design problems before he introduced them to the fleet. Wessex only had five when the model was discontinued, but I do not remember any problems other than with the brakes. Neither 927 nor 928 were registered until the start of the 1966 season. They were fitted with the identical Leyland 0.400 engine as in the Leyland Tiger Cub, but it was mounted vertically at the front and not under the floor. When this engine was laid flat, as

950 on layover somewhere. It is almost certain that this coach was being deployed on express services and awaiting the return, because the labels are still attached to the screen.

947 WAE when new, traversing the Tramways Centre, Bristol, with Bert Hook, a no. 1 tour driver, at the wheel.

BHU 937C. Note the different paint treatment of the second batch and the 'Wessex' cut-out *(below)* on the lower back panel, which this one seems to have retained.

This alloy fretwork cutting was placed on the lower near and off-side rear panels of each side of the second delivery of Fireflys. As I remember it was removed at the first repaint, which explains why I have an example in my possession.

Middle and below: Contrasting styles: these two Bedford VAM 5s are from the same delivery. The top picture shows the Duple (Northern) style and 931 is a Hendon body. 935 would have been registered in late 1965 and 931 probably not until Easter 1966 – hence the different suffix.

in the Tiger Cub, it was relatively quiet, but when placed upright at the front end of a VAL, it had a very distinctive growl. However, it certainly proved it was man enough for the job. It was the practice that all new coaches went to the no. 1 tour drivers every season, and it was that driver who collected his own coach from Hendon (these two VALs never did extended tours). The driver who was to have had 928 was either on holiday or off sick, and Bill Jones asked if I would like to go in his place to collect it. I started from Hendon, round the North Circular – all was going well. There was, of course, no motorway then, so we came down the A4. By the time I got to Reading I must have relaxed a bit. I thought that I had got used to this new innovation, power steering. Now, the operation of the early power steering rams were not as sophisticated as those of today. The driver had to activate the system. To go right a gentle turn on the wheel was all that was needed and the ram would activate, but the vehicle would not self-centre of its own accord as is done today. It needed a slight help to tell it to return to a straight line – and I did not give that help, so at the cemetery roundabout by The Jack of Both Sides in Reading it kept on going right. This was an elongated island and I jumped the kerb of the roundabout. That woke me up, and it never happened again. The good thing about it was that I was not in Bill's sight so he never knew, but I did get some stick from the following drivers, who were not too keen on a jumped-up staff driver in their midst anyway.

The VAL gave a very comfortable ride due to the low centre of gravity and, with the advent of the motorways, they were sold on their added safety in the event of a tyre burst. The theory was that the coach would continue to drive normally and to be brought to a controlled stop. I cannot recall a VAL of ours ever suffering such an occurrence. The downside of this was the fact that with the small sixteen-inch wheels came small brake drums, and, although the shoe-width was increased, the linings were very prone to wear and overheating, causing serious brake fades. For this reason most VALs, including the Wessex vehicles, were supplied with an exhaust brake and/or electric retarders. Wessex had both systems.

Drivers were generally allocated a vehicle at the start of a season or at the commencement of their employment. They were fully responsible for that vehicle until the company chose to upgrade them to a (possibly) better one. A driver could be called upon to drive any vehicle if the situation demanded, but, as the coaches grew in size with later deliveries, there was a more selective system of choosing which drivers were allowed to drive the larger vehicles. The VALs in particular were pretty well off limits to everyone except the allocated drivers, and the 45-seaters were not available to any but trusted and reliable drivers.

The first two VALs were well accepted, and two senior drivers had one apiece. Bus 927 went to Norman Sykes and 928 to 'Greg' Gregory. These two drivers

The two VAL 14s from the first delivery.

were entirely different in style. Greg was the fastest driver on the company. If you ran with Greg and arranged to meet somewhere he had always drunk his tea by the time you arrived, but he was a super chap and remained a 'no. 1' driver up to the time of his retirement. Norman on the other hand was a 'plodder', he never appeared to hurry and was never in a flap, but he always arrived on time. He and I did a winter football job to London one Saturday. I was young and, looking back now, a fast driver. We left Bristol, stopped at The Golden Arrow cafe near Marlborough and I left first – flat out up the A4, through Reading into Maidenhead with no sign of Norman in the mirror. I ran down the hill to the lights at Maidenhead, and there was Norman about ten vehicles behind me. Norman was the only driver who could go a full season and beyond with no attention to the brakes on the VAL. He did not use them that often, always on the gearbox and the Telma retarder. He was a fantastic driver of the old school. Greg, on the other hand, would have two or three relines through a season, but to be fair most drivers would have done. Norman never used his handbrake when parked – always left the vehicle in gear, first or reverse in the opposite direction of the slope – and I still do the same. His proven theory was that the hot brake drums contracted to the shape of the shoes when cooling, causing ovality of the drums, and this ovality could be felt by slightly pulling up the handbrake with the vehicle in motion – not with Norman's coach. I digress.

In 1967 five more VAM/Viscounts came in (MHU 921/925F). In 1968 another VAL, now known as the VAL 70 and fitted with Bedford's own 7.66L engine, arrived. With this delivery there were also five VAM 70s, and the six were numbered MHU926F (the VAL) and MHU 920-916F (the VAMs). The larger

7.66L engine was now fitted to the VAM 70 also. It was at that point that I left Wessex to further my employment elsewhere, but I never lost my interest in this company and still did some part time driving later to keep my badge going.

In 1970 the only other VAL70 was delivered together with four VAM70s (VHT 911H to 915H). In 1971 four YRQs arrived (AHT 907 to 910J). The YRQ was the first of the under-floor engined vehicles, with the engine mounted upright in the middle of the chassis. This was the 466 engine. 1972 saw the arrival of ten YRQs, numbered EAE 906K to EAE 902K and EHW 901 to 896K. The last vehicles purchased by Wessex Coaches Ltd one YRT and five YRQs in 1973, numbered LAE 890L to 895L.

Where the nearside view of any of the tour coaches is shown, you will note a flip-top, chromed box affixed to the lower window rail at about the centre point of the vehicle. I believe that this was a Clifton Greys/Ernie Andrews innovation, and was fitted to all vehicles used on tour workings. The reason for this was that all the glasses covering what were intended by the bodybuilders to be destination boxes were lettered across the front of every vehicle, and so, when the coach was lined up in Anchor Road, no one would know where it was going. The box was used to house a small black plate lettered with the day's destination. The driver collected the applicable plate from either the office or the garage, together with his trip-loading chart, and placed it in the box to be removed by the traffic superintendent as the vehicle was pulling out of Anchor Road. The plate was then returned to the garage.

About 1969 the lettering of the vehicle was modified to include 'Wessex of Bristol' on the forward side panels of each vehicle.

For anyone doing the numbers, this was a total of 123 Bedford/Duple products in twenty-five years. I would have thought that the size of purchase should have received some acknowledgment in either Bedford's or Duple's advertising, but to my knowledge, this has never happened. I often wonder why the model-makers have also passed this company over. Surely an AEC or Daimler Duple from Corgi, or even a Bedford SB based on one of Feltham's or Wessex from EFE should at least have represented this once fine concern, and would have promised a satisfactory guarantee in numbers sold.

I have gone to great lengths to give you some background regarding the new vehicles, but, to me, the second-hand acquisitions and the reasons for them are far more interesting. I remember some interesting happenings to some of these coaches, and I hope that you find some of them as amusing as I do now looking back. The early second-hand coach acquisitions included many Daimlers. Some of these purchases were intended for contract buses, but the tidier ones were used to replace older vehicles both at Chard and Bristol on front-line coach duties. Chard was the graveyard. I will explain more about the Chard operation later.

This page: Nearside and Offside views of RHT 920G, a 1968 VAM 70.

EHW 899K. *Below:* EHW 896K at Salisbury.

LAE 892L from the
final batch of vehicles
purchased, pictured
outside Clifton Road
garage. In 1973-4 this was
the Bristol City FC coach.
See further comments
at end of the chapter
regarding this vehicle.

KXY 485 was a regular
weekend visitor to
Kingswood and worked
hard on express duties.

BBV 418 was the coach
that is mentioned on page
125 as being re-furbished
for the North Devon tours.

Their coaches were old, but they were immaculate, inside and out, everything would be polished – the aluminium mouldings glistened like chrome. If one of our coaches failed anywhere along the south coast, we would ring Chard and one of their vehicles would go out to recover the passengers Our coach would then be repaired at Chard. The replacement vehicle would return to Bristol that night and work a tour back through Chard next morning to collect the Bristol vehicle. Never can I remember anyone having to go out to a Chard vehicle. They just never broke down. Len Osborne was the foreman fitter there.

On summer weekends as many as twenty of these 'old bangers' would be brought to Bristol on a Friday night. Drivers would park up and sleep in their vehicles in the yard at Kingswood, and early on Saturday they would be despatched to wherever needed on Associated Motorways work – occasionally not getting home until Monday or Tuesday of the following week. Sometimes maybe five or six coaches would be detailed to work the early services out of Victoria to Bristol, Birmingham or Plymouth. These would travel to London on the Friday night. Chard operated mainly Daimlers and AECs in my time, with bodywork by Duple, Plaxton's, Gurney-Nutting, Burlingham or Harrington. One such Daimler, in the late 50s, was refurbished by Duple and retained for the North Devon tour from Bristol because it was only 7ft 6in wide. This particular vehicle BBV 418 was purchased second-hand in 1959, and gave another seven years of good service ending its life at Wylfa Power Station. It had a notice in the cab for the benefit of the North Devon tour, which read, 'AT THE TOP OF COUNTISBURY HILL <u>STOP</u>. Engage 1ˢᵗ gear – select reverse'. This meant that the driver would be travelling down this 1:4 hill in first gear, but if the vehicle started to 'run away', he could press the gear change pedal to engage reverse, which was already selected. I never tried this but was reliably informed that if a driver did so the vehicle would come to a juddering stop and slowly creep backwards.

We used to run a Saturday service from Bristol to the holiday camp at Westward Ho in North Devon for the Co-op, using two coaches. One Saturday the 'phone went at about 1pm. It was from a part-time driver called Bert Masters, who was on the service that day with a Daimler (coach). He was crying. I said to him, 'whatever's the matter Bert?' He said, 'I've broken my leg, I've broken my leg!' I thought that he was kidding but he was not. In the end I had to go down in my car and bring the coach back. The pedal had come out of the floor, and, although he had not broken his leg, he did himself a fair bit of damage and was in considerable pain. He drove my car back, and I had to return with coach and passengers. The way to (hope) to avoid this kickback was to rest the inside edge of the left foot on the left hand edge of the pedal and to hold that pedal down for a count of three. There were no 'racing changes' with a Daimler.

As I have said most second-hand purchases up to 1962-3 were to cover the power-station contracts, but in 1963 there was another very significant reason for a number of second-hand coaches to be obtained for the coaching fleet. The first batch of Bristol RELH coaches was supposed to have been delivered to the erstwhile BOC in March 1963. Due to a strike at Lowestoft, the first one (only) was not actually delivered until September '63, and the rest did not arrive until the start of the 1964 season. The consequence of this delay was that BOC were unable to fulfil their commitments to Associated Motorways, and Wessex was expected to fill the void as the main contractor to BOC, so a fair few heavyweights were purchased. As is probably very well known, that first RE was the first production model, 861 UAE (2115).

Because of the late arrival of the Bristol REs to BOC, Bill Jones purchased a number of 'heavyweight' coaches in 1962-3 to fill the gap. Wessex was the main contractor to BOC, who were liable to ring at ten minutes' notice for a coach to be sent to either Bristol or Bath Bus Stations for 'Express' work. Some of these additions were worn out; others were in fair condition. I remember being caught out with one on several occasions. I was a staff driver and technically one of the last out, but at short notice anything could happen, and I would be left with whatever vehicle happened to be in the garage. One Easter Sunday afternoon I had covered the 'pick ups' for the 2.30pm afternoon tours and taken the passengers into Anchor Road in an AEC. It was my half day, and I had arranged to get home as early as possible and take ''er indoors' out for a couple of hours. I dropped the passengers and returned to the garage at Kingswood – it was now about 2.50pm. I parked up and called into the office to say that I was off, but Raymond said, 'Oh no, take anything that's available – you are on the 2.25pm London service out of Bath.' Now Bath was another 25 minutes away, so I was already a projected fifty minutes late leaving Bath. We had no 'phone at home at that time; there was no way that I could contact my wife, but was assured that someone would let her know that I would be home *much* later. To cut a long story short, I got home at 2.30am to find a very tearful and distressed wife sat wondering what could possibly have happened to her beloved, as no one had let her know until the late evening, and did not tell her where I was gone. If I remember rightly this was the point where I decided that this was to be my last season.

NRO 510 was one of these late acquisitions – an AEC Regal IV with a Burlingham Seagull body and centre entrance door. It was in a smart condition and very tidy inside, having been previously owned by Brunt's of Hatfield. It went straight into the paint shop, was painted and lettered within two days of purchase and went out on the road earning money. However, the first time we used it on the following Saturday we put it on express Brighton, and it was discovered that the block was cracked. Just imagine the poor driver. Centre entrance and the radiator filler cap is inside the coach, in front of the passengers' feet, on the front nearside bulkhead. He had to carry five-gallon drums of water and, every fifty miles or so, get the drum from the boot, bring it into the coach to top the radiator up and then get the drum refilled. It ran for a couple of weeks like that with a part-timer, Bill Bowrey, using it. It was quite a pleasant vehicle to drive, after the problem had been remedied. The other one that Bill bought at the same time was another Seagull PPE 463. This one was not so tidy inside so the body shop spent a day tidying it. This coach had moquette seats with rexine infills, which were in very poor state, so the body shop staff painted them with cream gloss paint. Come Saturday morning the paint had not dried so they put newspaper all across the back seat and passengers had to sit on that.

Having said that please, dear reader, do not think that some matters were slipshod. I must point out that all vehicles were not only subject to annual inspection by the 'ministry', but also, when any second-hand vehicle was purchased and it had come from another traffic area (as these latter two would have done), it had to be inspected by an engineer from The Western Traffic Area to ensure its safety before being allowed to operate. It could not be used until this inspection had taken place and the required paperwork had been issued. This usually entailed a lengthy pit inspection, as well as the interior safety features. No coach was allowed on the road without the 'legal writing' being painted on the lower nearside panels. This had to include the operator's trading name and address, the name of the Company secretary and the ULW of the vehicle. Prior to the 1968 Traffic Act, rules and standards were not quite as rigid as in later years, as this and subsequent Acts demanded.

NKH 2 was a Plaxton Venturer on an AEC Regal IV weighing in at 9.5 tons unladen. This was at one time a Chard-based vehicle, but the Chard drivers did not like it and refused to do the Kingswood pick-ups on day or afternoon tours with this one, because it was too heavy to pull around the streets of our area with no power steering. Therefore, I had to do the pick-ups when it did a tour from our end. However they got around the Devon and Dorset lanes with this one I do not know. This particular vehicle was eventually transferred back to Kingswood and I did a few jobs with it – I rather liked it. I took it to London one Sunday afternoon on 'express' and it performed a treat. After much deliberation it was at last agreed that on peak Saturdays we should keep one vehicle in reserve, to cover 'eventualities'. For a time this vehicle was the real 'dog' of the fleet – EF 8766, a Maudsley Marathon 35-seater that had had a full front conversion at some time. Now this thing needed as much room to stop as a fully laden oil tanker in mid-Atlantic. If it had not been called out by twelve noon on a Saturday it could be safely assumed that most coaches were now pretty near to their destinations, so Wessex got it out on the road earning money. Frank Davis at Colston Avenue booking office would write up a board advertising an afternoon tour from Anchor Road *only*, and old EF would be put either on that tour or, if BOC 'phoned for an extra coach, it would be put on 'express' for Associated Motorways (who were the forerunners of National Express for those who do not know). One particular staff driver (not me) directly refused to take EF out one Saturday; mind you, it was a very poor advert for the company to use anyway.

It does illustrate the point though that a driver really earned his money in those days, without all of the fancy innovations fitted to modern coaches today. This reminds me of another situation: drivers were instructed that, if they were going to break down, they were to make sure that they did it near a pub or a café. This would give the fitters time to get to the casualty, without upsetting the passengers too much. Wessex never hired to cover breakdowns, but always sent another coach and a fitter from Bristol or Chard – no matter where or what time of night. We had a coach once in Switzerland with a blown engine, a Firefly it was. One hundred miles away (in Austria), was another identical coach on a two-day layover. The office contacted the second driver; he drove into Switzerland to meet the first one and they swapped coaches. The second coach was used to pick up the casualties' passengers the next morning and the other was repaired and sent back to carry on its original journey as if nothing had happened. The passengers were totally unaware of a change of vehicle. Two fitters went out with an engine in the back of the van and changed it on the car park. At that time Wessex did not encourage continental work and did very little of it. In the '60s Bedford 'middleweight' vehicles were not really up to this type of arduous tour.

Only three Bedford SB5 41-seaters were bought second-hand during the 1963 season. THR 240, 821 CUP and 157 ALH each came in with Super Vega bodies and the larger 330 engines. We had these at Kingswood and they were very nice vehicles. In 1965 came 6964 NU, an SB5 with a Duple Bella Vega body. This was the only Bella Vega owned and reputed to be the fastest vehicle in the fleet at the time – for whatever reason, I do not know, 'Ginger' Hallett refused to give it up for a new one and they kept it at Clifton. In 1963 Bill Jones bought six Regal IVs with Windover Kingsway bodies. Mechanically, as I remember, these were OK, but, oh, that ugly-looking body! The vehicles were new to Timpson's of London, but came to us from a dealer in Cheshire. We used them for a few weekends on Express Services and sent them to Chard at the first opportunity. They only lasted two years with the group anyway.

From what has been said already, the reader will have gathered that Chard was the unfortunate dustbin. Kingswood was half way to the dustbin, but the last stop was always Chard. Clifton had the new, Kingswood had the displacements, and last came Chard. The reason for this was as follows. Chard was undoubtedly the poor relation; it was what would be called in modern parlance today, a 'low-cost operation'. They survived on lots of contract work with a few afternoon or short day-trips as a seaside operator from Bridport and West Bay to maybe Weymouth or Lyme Regis. Employment at Chard was generally hard to find, and therefore the Chard drivers were mainly older men – but very conscientious and some had been employed for many years. They were generally happy with their lot, because the older coaches that they were driving were a very great improvement upon the vehicles operated by the original company. The drivers were most appreciative of the weekend work when they were brought to Bristol. Chard survived on year-round contract work with schools and workers contracts, for which some vehicles were out-based at Crewkerne, Axminster, Bridport and as far away as Bridgwater. Some inherited stage-carriage services were also operated.

Kingswood could probably not have survived on its own. Kingswood relied upon Clifton for an almost daily allocation of work, to provide work for the number of drivers it employed. As an overflow for Clifton, we had a lot more unmanned coaches based with us at Kingswood than would have been necessary had we been self-supporting. We had nowhere near the number of drivers as we had coaches, so we had to rely on part-timers at busy times for these vehicles. I remember on many occasions running around, knocking on doors, trying to find drivers to come in at a minute's notice. We had a list of probably thirty part-timers, but it was when all else failed that I had to go out – not that I minded very much. I used to enjoy the driving but the problem then was, I usually got the dregs of the work and finished up driving the dregs of the fleet also. Sometimes the situation would arise that they had spare vehicles at Clifton and no drivers. Clifton had their list of part-timers as we did, but, if we had exhausted our list or they had exhausted theirs, I had to go to Clifton to collect a coach (usually a much better machine than we had) and cover work from Clifton. We had good front-line vehicles at Kingswood which could be sent on any job of any standard, but we also had older coaches. We had our own private-hire work, most of which was inherited from customers of Feltham's, plus we had good school contracts, but we relied on Clifton to give us more. Day tours were all charted at Whiteladies Road. George would look at the loadings and say, 'There's more on that load from Kingswood area than Clifton – give it to Kingswood'. Maybe a private hire, booked through Clifton, would be starting from our side of town that would come to us. If there were twenty vehicles required on a private hire that job would be shared, maybe fifteen to five, in favour of Clifton. George, or someone from that office, would telephone daily at about 5pm every day with our allocation of work for tomorrow. It was the job of either Raymond or me to

To illustrate the standard of the Extended Tours I show here a copy of the 1962 leaflet as provided to intending passengers. It will be noted that the standard of hotels used was very high on each tour, and that the cost included full-board accommodation and hotel staff tips. This must have been exceedingly good value even in the impoverished 1960s.

Fifty-one years separate the two pictures with a 1921 Maid of the Mountains Daimler in the above picture and EHW 899K, a 1972 Bedford YRQ, below.

interlace that work with our own commitments, as would be done in any busy traffic office today. We then produced the duty sheet for tomorrow and pinned it up in the garage for the incoming drivers to read.

The legal ownership of vehicles was swapped back and forth between the fleets all of the time as PSV Circle records will show, but many of these changes were paper transactions only for the purpose of the balance sheets. In the heyday of my time with the company, I think that Wessex must have owned well in excess of 200 vehicles at any one time. I don't believe that anyone ever counted them, except maybe Company Secretary Mr Bellamy – and probably in his sleep as well.

It will be noted from the accompanying photos that you have to look very hard to find any accident damage on any vehicle (except maybe the contract fleet). Presentation was a theme that was strongly upheld by the company. Even

University Rag Week, 1964. The entire fleet would have been utilised for various activities during Rag Week every year in March, culminating with this huge procession through Clifton and Central Bristol. 946 WAE, one of that year's Fireflys leads the procession – most likely with Bert Foote driving. The students would have filled the coach with the balloons and George's and Raymond's children would be in there somewhere. My Fair Lady was showing at the 'Whiteladies Cinema. Lower pic is passing Whiteladies Road office and the upper is passing through the Broadmead shopping area.

if the body shop had to work all night, no vehicle was allowed on the road with battle-scars visible.

I was asked what, if any, service vehicles were used by the company. From the mid- '60s onward the de-roofed Daimler CVD6 was used as a mobile workshop for running repairs mainly on the contract sites, although this particular vehicle would have been no use whatsoever for a long-distance tow. For that purpose, in my time, a seven-ton Bedford S-type would have been used, but that particular vehicle had very little usage in this role. At one time I remember a 15cwt. Ford Thames van, and there was an Austin A40 van, lettered and painted in company colours that was used as a runabout by the fitting staff.

CHAPTER 10

The Personalities

One cannot tell these stories of Wessex Coaches Ltd without writing another book about the personalities – those past and those with whom I worked. These people were the lifeblood of the company, and some do deserve further mention here. Many drivers and 'inside' staff had been with Wessex for a considerable number of years, and each would be equally well regarded. Each played his own part to the success and growth of the company. I tender my sincere apologies to those loyal servants whose names I do not mention.

I'll start with Ted Jones, the founder of Morning Star. At some time in his life he worked as a docker at Avonmouth Docks, and received a bravery award for diving in to the water and rescuing a seaman trapped between the dock wall and the ship. On another occasion he saw a horse and cart reverse into the Feeder Canal – the cart went in first and pulled the horse in with it. With no more ado he dived in and freed the struggling horse of its harness, thus enabling it to be pulled out. For his actions he received a humane award from the RSPCA or its equivalent. He was, apparently, a very tough cookie. He died in 1942. Ted had four sons and two daughters. Each of the sons worked for their father and each fell out with him over the years. George (G.J.) was the eldest, Bill came next, then Charlie and the youngest was Jim. I know that George, Bill and Jim, although having left the business a few times in between, were each lorry-driving for Ted at the start of the war. Jim had worked for his father pre-war as a driver, but joined the Merchant Navy at the outbreak and was allowed to return to the business upon the death of his father. As a driver he would have been in a 'reserved occupation'. He was a long-distance driver carrying essential supplies for the duration, and left before 1947 to set up his own, very successful engineering business.

George and Bill had driven both lorries and coaches prior to the war and continued to do so, although I imagine that the pressure had intensified after the outbreak of war, when all transport movements would have been controlled by the Ministry of War Transport. Locally, these movements were controlled from an office in Avonmouth Docks, the idea being to co-ordinate journeys and thereby save precious fuel. Ted had died in 1942, so I would imagine that George would have operated in a much more administrative role from then on (and probably before also). I know from my conversations with Bill that he personally drove for most of the war, but also coped with a lot of the maintenance and vehicle repairs of both the wartime coach/bus fleet and the transport fleet also. Both George and Bill were certainly kept very busy on a day-to-day basis, and I am sure that a lot of midnight oil must have been used. The transport fleet was sold off in early 1947 prior to the nationalisation of all transport fleets operating under A or B licences for hire and reward. Own account, C licence holders were exempt, but could not carry goods other than their own.

By the time that I joined Wessex George had all but retired; we never really saw much of him at Kingswood. He and Mrs Jones would visit Raymond and his family socially and that was about it. I certainly never got to know him in a business context. I am told that he kept in daily touch with Whiteladies Road and knew everything that happened, as it happened, and he would appear at Whiteladies Road only on the day of a Board Meeting. Mr Jones was very keen on horseracing – he owned a racehorse. He was also a Director of Bristol City FC in the early 1950s. I know that he used to watch afternoon horse racing on the television, 'phone his bookie, place a bet, and then go out to sit on the seat at the end of Eagle Road, Brislington, because he could not bear to watch the race. George had two sons, George (G.T.) and Raymond.

Now Bill was a different kettle of fish altogether – very much hands on, he would be in Clifton Road garage early almost every morning or else he would be on the road making his checkups – as I will explain. Bill Jones was G.J. Jones' younger brother and was a super chap, into his 60s when I joined, but a real old-timer. Bill was a founder member of the Western Section of The Institute of Road Transport Engineers, and his name often arises between the old-timers now even though he has been dead for over thirty-five years. To me, and to older members of staff, Bill was always Uncle Bill, as Raymond and George always called him. He and I had many conversations where he would tell me stories of how he and his mate, Bob Major, driving steam lorries on general haulage work across the country used to chop down peoples' wooden fences in the middle of the night to keep the fire going, and break into council yards to 'borrow' some oil. This employment was in the period(s) when he had fallen out with his father and went to work for Joseph Fish, as G.J. did also at various times. Joseph Fish is a now forgotten name (by some) and former operator of steam lorries in Bristol.

Bill could be firm; if a driver did something wrong affecting the mechanics of the vehicle he knew that he would get a rollicking from Bill, but it would soon be forgotten and Bill would be sat in the tearoom drinking tea with the offender in no time. Some mornings he would sit in the car park of the Queens Head pub at the top of Bedminster Down on the south side of Bristol and wait for the tour coaches to come up the hill. He would watch out for any vehicles emitting excessive smoke or not pulling too well, but also any driver not wearing his hat or maybe smoking a cigarette. This would be noted and Bill would be in the garage when they returned at night and have words with the drivers concerned. I believe that the law saying that a driver must not smoke whilst in control of a PCV stood even before the time of the July 2007 act banning smoking in enclosed premises and vehicles, although it was often ignored in the 1960s and before. Another of Bill's favourite spots was The Darlington Arms half way down Redhill on the right and a further seven miles out of town. This time he would park out of sight behind a wall and note the numbers of all the Wessex vehicles going down Redhill without changing down a gear; those drivers would also be on the carpet that night. Redhill is about 1:8 incline, and on what was the main road (A38) to the South Coast.

Bill was an engineer of the old brigade: he never had formal training but had learnt by hands-on experience – the hard way. He had a store at Clifton Road garage where he used to keep all his old 'bits'. Raymond tells me differently and says that his store was organised; as I remember it was anything but – everything was just thrown in and piled high. People used to ring Bill from all over the country for a Leyland gearbox, a Daimler fuel pump or maybe a Bedford OB drive shaft, and Bill would go to his store, dig down under a pile of starter motors, dynamos, pumps and even complete engines to find what he was looking for. He knew that it was there and, usually, exactly where. Bill's passion in life, after work and his family, was coarse fishing. He worked to his retirement but on the first day of the coarse fishing season, three months after he retired, he collapsed and died whilst fishing on Chew Valley Lake. Both Bill and G.J. Jones had come up the hard way, as did their father before them. Bill had no sons to follow him into the business.

Young George left school and went straight into the garage to learn the fitting side of the business. He was employed there until about 1956, when he was brought into the office at Whiteladies Road. Raymond, on the other hand, left school and had no real interest in the business, so, at the age of 14, he got himself a job as a tea boy in Thrissell Engineering – just down the road from the family home. He was called up for his National Service and served in Egypt, but came back to the business, older and wiser, and joined the family firm. He served in all departments and in 1961, upon the takeover of Feltham's business became General Manager of that department at Kingswood where I joined him shortly after. Raymond was the younger of the two sons and was more an office type than George. Raymond was one of only a couple of senior staff members who had never taken a PSV test and was therefore unable to drive a loaded coach (I think that he knew what he was doing!). I sometimes used to take him with me on afternoon workers contracts in the winter and let him drive the empty coach, but he was never keen to get his licence. I am still in regular contact with him and his wife.

L.W. Andrews had passed away around 1960. The founder of Clifton Greys, he was ninety years old (I believe), but had remained active up to his death. L.W. had two sons, Bert and Ernie. Sadly, Ernie passed away in 1962. He collapsed and died in his car whilst on his way to visit Duples at Hendon. I knew very little of Ernie Andrews personally; in fact, I only remember meeting him once but was told that he was a stickler for detail. He was a gentleman, and a disciplinarian. Sometimes he would stand talking to a driver, maybe in Anchor Road or at the garage. Whilst talking he would have his back to the coach and his hand up under the wheel arch, and if he could pull dirt from under the wing, he would send that driver back to the garage to clean his coach again. The vehicles had to be spotless, and the 'uniform' policy for the drivers to wear a white shirt, black tie, a white knee length coat and a peaked cap with a white cover, between Easter and the first weekend in October, probably originated with Clifton Greys. This was, however, also the norm for drivers of most companies prior to the war and as far back as the early 1920s, but not many operators enforced the practise after the war as in the case of Clifton Greys/Wessex drivers, where the coat and hat were supplied by the company, together with the white hat cover. Apart from the hat itself, these items would be exchanged for freshly laundered ones each Monday morning, but the white shirt and black tie the driver provided himself – and woe betide anyone with a grubby shirt. This practise was continued and strictly enforced to the very end of Wessex, although it was eventually realised that it was nothing but torture to wear a heavy linen coat, behind glass, on a steaming hot summer's day. In about 1970, a short grey nylon coat replaced the full-length white one. Bert Andrews looked after the stores and purchasing at Clifton Road and worked all his life for the company before he retired, shortly after Ernie's death. I never had the pleasure of meeting Bert. Several members of the Andrews family retained their shareholdings until the demise of the company.

When the company was formed in 1948 there were four particular employees who appear to have been regarded as 'senior'. The first of these was the aforementioned Mr Bellamy. He had worked for Clifton Greys, in an office position, since leaving school. Mr Bellamy was given the position of Traffic Manager. The next was Alec. Lusher. Alec had been employed during the war by the Ministry of War Transport, and at the end of the war was employed by

Morning Star. He was made Company Secretary upon the formation of Wessex in 1948. Within a few months, for whatever reason, the two appointments were reversed and the two gentlemen swapped jobs and titles. Quite logical really considering that Mr Bellamy was from an accountancy background and Alec was an experienced transport man. Alec became Traffic Manager and Mr B. became Company Secretary, a position that he held until the company was finally dissolved. Alec unfortunately died in the office one Saturday morning in September 1957. Shortly after their appointments, each was offered the option of 5,000 shares as a reward for their loyalty. From Maple Leaf came Frank Davis and Harry Lewis (more about these later) but both held positions of authority within the traffic department.

Mr Bellamy became Company Secretary in 1950 with his office at Whiteladies Road. He was a very dour man. I am told that he started for L.W. Andrews when he was a boy and worked his way up the ladder. This was the only job that he had ever had; indeed, he worked in the same office for all of his working life. One very seldom saw him smile – let alone laugh. He spoke very few words unless you went to him for money, and then he would give every reason under the sun for not giving you any. I will give you an example: I was allowed four gallons of petrol a week to run my own car for the company's benefit. I had a Ford Zephyr doing about 28-30mpg and I used it to collect passengers, visit the booking agents on a weekly basis and to fetch and carry as required. One Saturday a family of four were left behind at Bedminster Down on period bookings, and I had to pick them up and take them to Torquay, a round trip of about 240 miles. The following Monday I went to Clifton Road to fill up with petrol and was told that, because I had had my 'ration' on the previous Friday, they would have to contact Mr Bellamy. The garage staff rang him and he said, 'No, he can't have any petrol, he's had his four gallons for the week', and that I had to take the rough with the smooth, quite wrongly implying that there were weeks when I did not use my 'ration'. No way would he change his mind; I confronted him and told my story but it was to no avail, he would not relent. Luckily Harry Lewis bailed me out and I filled up on his name for the next few weeks so Mr Bellamy was not quite as clever as he thought.

For all of that, he was a great thinker, and credit must be given to the man for the way in which he managed the financial affairs of the company. When talking to him one could watch him sit back and ponder before he answered a question or offered his opinion – he was a great thinker. To me at least, he was *always* Mr Bellamy, but behind his back we called him 'Syd'. He was secretary of the Passenger Vehicle Operators Association, Western Section, and a very well known and respected man throughout the industry. Nancy Hough was his secretary who he later married – after each of them had retired. Mr Bellamy was appointed a director of the Company in 1970. As Traffic Manager, Alec was also very well respected and older drivers would often mention his name in a reverend fashion when talking of old times. I believe that in his ten-year tenure he made many policy decisions which moulded the later operations of the company. Alec collapsed in the office one Saturday morning and was pronounced dead on arrival at the hospital.

Wessex was a very personal and friendly business: every one referred to and addressed George and Raymond by their Christian names, and they in turn knew the Christian name of every driver employed. Although older members of staff referred to him as George, to me Mr G.J. Jones was always 'Mr', even when I used to visit his house socially. From 1957 George ran the traffic side of the business from the Whiteladies Road Office, and drivers would refer to him as 'young George'. All tour and excursion bookings came through the Whiteladies Road Office, and all-day and extended tour booking charts were kept there as well as details of the private hire work booked through that office. The Private Hire department was a separate autonomous department run by Stan Savage (more of Stan later). At Kingswood, we maintained all booking charts for the period bookings and had our own private hire department. There must have been at least sixty booking agents spread across and around the city, and two to three full-time booking clerks at Whiteladies Road to take their calls, but the 'phones were answered by anyone and everyone in that office. If you were passing through and a 'phone was ringing, you answered it. It was a very hectic place during the season, with several phones ringing at the same time. Agencies were located in corner shops, mainly newsagents, and near every booking agency would be a pick up point for the intending passenger.

The Traffic Superintendent in direct contact with the Clifton drivers, and the liaison man to sort out the problems, was Harry Lewis. I do not think that Harry ever had an official title, but that is what it would have been today. Harry had worked as a driver for Cliff Jordan at Maple Leaf for several years before the amalgamation, and had come into Wessex with that company. Now, Harry was a one off. I do not think I ever saw Harry lose his temper. I do not think that anyone, directors, drivers or passengers ever had cause to say a bad word about Harry. He was a quiet and reserved man; not many knew anything about his personal life, but he was a Gentleman with a capital G. He would walk across the garage with his lips pursed to whistle but very little sound ever came out. He would have a perpetual smile on his face, but if he was walking toward you, you had a fair idea that he wanted something done. Sometimes it would be a seemingly impossible task, but, with his manner, Harry was never refused. Harry would come up to you and say, 'Morning sweetheart, everything OK with you', everyone was sweetheart, 'wouldn't do me a favour, would you?' and you have agreed without knowing it. A driver could be hurrying and sweating to get his coach ready, when along would come Harry. 'I've got two left behind at Sea Mills. You wouldn't mind taking my car and picking 'em up would you? Thanks for that sweetheart; I'll remember you at Christmas'. He would then turn and walk away. Before you could argue – it was done. Harry always remembered to whom he owed favours and returned them gladly if you had a problem. Harry never *told* anyone to do anything – he always *asked*, and he had a fantastic personality. There is a funny thing about Harry, which I have probably only just realised. As I have said, everyone was on first name terms but, if Harry was talking to a driver and referred to George, Raymond, Bill or Syd Bellamy, he would always refer to them as *Mr* Jones or *Mr* Bellamy (the latter was Mr to most people anyway). It was Harry's way, and his polite respect.

Harry also dealt directly with the passengers. Bearing in mind that we had tours leaving Anchor Road At 7.15am, 8am, 8.45am, 10am and 2.30pm, and assuming an average of 60 coaches a day spread over these departures and each with an average capacity of 38-41, means a figure in excess of 2,000 passengers in the course of a day that he was dealing with, placating any passengers who were not happy along the way – and there were always some. This he did admirably and with a smile on his face.

I recall seeing, probably in 1952 while working at Cathedral Garage, a line of Wessex coaches stretching, literally, from the Hotwell Road end of Anchor Road, past our workshop and back toward the Centre as far as I could see. I would not like to hazard a guess to the numbers involved but there were certainly very many coaches there on that particular Saturday morning. This memory alone illustrates the boom years of the coaching industry. By the time that I joined it things had calmed a little and by 1962 car ownership was increasing and people were able to get about more independently but the coach business was still thriving all the same.

On a peak Sunday in particular we could have maybe twenty coaches or more lined up for various destinations at one time. The busiest were the 8.45 and 2.30pm departures, and when it was really busy there may have been two or three of us helping Harry and Frank Davis to sort it all out. It was unusual if all coaches had not departed within ten minutes of their specified time. Sometimes passengers did not turn up, sometimes we would be overbooked, but Harry always sorted it to everyone's satisfaction. These extras would stand by the railings of the railway goods yard alongside Anchor Road and Harry would be buzzing about. He would say, 'All right sweetheart, I've got two for Torquay, that OK?' He would take their money, issue the tickets and hand them over to the driver. Couple of minutes later he would shuffle people around and find more empty seats.

Long before I started, so the story went, Harry had the line of coaches one morning and several people had turned up on the off chance of finding seats to anywhere. Now, as I have said, these were the heydays of the '50s when everyone wanted to ride. On this particular day, he had fixed every one up bar two – a young couple. He went back to them and said, 'Look, I've got just two seats left. One is on that coach and one is on this one. You will be all right; you will see each other when you get there, that OK?' That was agreed. Apparently, the young man had the money and she had the sandwiches, (or vice versa). The two coaches pulled away and everyone was happy. When the young woman's coach got to the first refreshment stop at Warminster she had got out and was standing at the back of the coach looking anxiously down the road. The driver saw her stood there and asked if she was all right. She said 'Oh yes. I am just waiting for the other coach.' 'What other coach?' says the driver. 'The one that left Anchor Road with us' she says. The driver said, 'Oh you won't see that coach, he's gone to Torquay, we're going to Southsea.' The driver got on the 'phone to Harry and told him what had happened. Everyone but Harry thought that it was hilarious, but he waited until that night and met the coaches into Bristol. These two got out and were going to tear Harry to pieces, but he calmed them down. He gave them their money back there and then and told them that they would never ever pay for another trip on Wessex Coaches as long as they lived. Apparently these two got married, had children, and, for several years afterward, were still riding free of charge by contacting Harry first. That is a perfectly true story of Harry Lewis.

Having said all of that, Harry was not the man to get on the wrong side of – he was an enforcer of the company rules and would pull a man aside and tell him quietly if he saw rules being broken. The main ones were:

1. A driver must present himself and his vehicle in a smart condition at all times, and be properly dressed in white coat and hat.

2. The driver was not to be seen smoking in the presence of passengers and certainly not smoke whilst driving.

3. All blinds on the screens above the driver's head had to be pulled back at all times. These quarter light windows were there for the passengers' benefit and his view had not to be obstructed. Never mind about the poor driver roasting away in the heat.

4. When on 'Express' work, adhesive labels were stuck to the front screen. These had to be totally removed as soon as possible. No remnants whatsoever were to remain, especially on a tour coach. This was probably Harry's 'pet' aversion.

5. And finally, goodness help the man who 'swept out' and left a mess on the garage floor!

One Saturday we had two coaches on afternoon tour to Malvern Hills and British Camp, and we 'lost' the second coach. I had covered the pick-ups from our side of the city in the eight-seat Bedford Dormobile, and had taken the people into the pick-up point for 2.30pm. Frank Davis, another staff driver, had the first coach and left with about thirty-five people remaining on the pavement and no coach. No mobile 'phones in those days of course; there was no way that we could contact the driver – and he had certainly not bothered to contact us. As I have said previously, it had been agreed that we would keep one coach spare every Saturday for such an eventuality. This was George's decision, but I think that it only happened on a few Saturdays and certainly not this one. The coach that we had lost was returning empty from Birmingham, having covered a journey for Associated Motorways, and should have been back at about 2.00pm. Harry pacified the customers; they were eating out of his hand – he even stopped a passing ice-cream van and bought an ice cream for everyone. He made several 'phone calls and, at about 3.30pm he said to me, 'Come with me sweetheart.'

I jumped into his car, but he would not tell me where we were going. We finished up at Lawrence Hill BOC depot. An inspector took us across the yard to a line of redundant Greyhound coaches, LL6Bs (Queen Mary's), and said, 'Take your pick'. I think that we had it free of charge so it was not a 'hired vehicle'. Harry said, 'there you are, you are Malvern Hills Coach 2'. I said, 'But Harry, I have never done this tour.' He said, 'Not to worry, they are nearly all Saturday regulars; the passengers will put you right if you get lost', and off we went. Now no one had ever told me that if you stopped an LL6B in overdrive 5th it would not come out again while stationary (not good driving practice anyway). I got to Gloucester Cross, stopped at the lights and now I was stuck. I just managed to get it rolling on the flat and got it out of fifth. By the end of that trip, I had become quite adept at changing gear with no clutch, because if there was one on this bus, it never worked for me. I remember that I made slow changes, I tried to make fast changes, I tried letting the revs die to tick-over, and I still did not win. Having said that I do not think that I made too bad a job of it, and the passengers cheered when we got back to Bristol. I did very well on tips that day and everyone was happy. Imagine that scenario nowadays!

When I took the coach back to Lawrence Hill and said about the lack of a clutch to the inspector, he told me that it was a scrapper and awaiting sale. I think that it was either NHY 947 or 948. The lost coach had had a rear axle problem on the A38 and the driver said that he could not find a 'phone box. There was a funny sequel to this story. This tour stopped at The Old Mill in Tewkesbury for tea and by the time I arrived, Frank was leaving. He put me right for the rest of the tour – up the A38, turn left for Upton on Severn, climb up to the station in Malvern and turn left, bear right and follow for the Wyche Cutting arriving at British Camp for half an hour stop – return via Ledbury. I duly got to British Camp, thinking that Frank was well on his way home by now. While I am stood there, in pulls Frank. He had got confused because of the new M50 motorway construction and got hopelessly lost. We laughed about that for a long time afterwards – I did not dare tell Harry.

Raymond and I were reminiscing recently and Ray said, 'You know, nobody is indispensible within a company, but if anything had happened to Harry Lewis, we would have needed two people to replace him' – and I would fully agree with that.

Frank Davis was Harry's sidekick, and they were great friends having worked together with Maple Leaf for years previous. Nothing like the temperament of Harry, in fact, he could be quite abrasive, but if you got the two together, they were like the *Two Ronnies* – they would have made a good television act. Harry (and drivers) would wind Frank up, tell him impossible stories, knowing that Frank could be made to believe anything. Frank was a super chap really, always ready to help if you were in trouble. The three of us were in Anchor Road one day and we were waiting for two passengers. Time's going on and we are a bit anxious. Harry, with his permanent smile, said to Frank, 'Do you remember them, thee's booked 'em' (Bristol Dialect). Frank says, 'I think I remember – North Country'. Harry said, 'The last time thee's said that they was Chinese.' Harry retired when the business was sold in 1974 and carried on working driving a minibus for the disabled for several years afterwards – such was Harry. Unfortunately, Frank passed away before the time of National takeover.

Frank was Harry's aide in checking out all tours, and deputised for Harry during his holidays etc. The rest of his time during the summer season was spent either in the booking office at Colston Avenue on The Tramways Centre, or looking after the booking agents around the city as I looked after the ones on the northern areas. This entailed collecting very large sums of cash in the season, paying in and banking with continual year-round contact with agents to ensure that they had sufficient advertising material etc. In this position one often became a personal friends with the agents as one visited them so often, always a cup of tea on the table and a friendly chat – I am sure that Frank would have agreed with this.

All Clifton drivers were ultimately responsible to George and Kingswood drivers were to Raymond. On the ladder in between would be Bill Jones, Harry Lewis, Frank Davis and myself.

Wessex produced a six-page leaflet twice a week in the busy periods from Easter to about mid-September, and at least once a week at other times listing the tours available over the next few days. These lists were prepared all the year round, and had to be delivered to the agents as soon as possible (see copy in later chapter). That was the job of Frank, myself and another long-time servant of Clifton Greys, Bill Hamilton.

Colston Avenue was a very busy booking office situated on one of the main thoroughfares of the City Centre, and accounted for a large slice of the tour and excursion clientele in the summer with passing trade from visitors. This office was situated in what must have been the most favoured location possible for its purpose, and all of the major city operators had an office within about 200 yards. All visitors to the city would have to pass this spot whilst sightseeing, and it is probably fair to say that 40% of all tour bookings came through this 'office'. It was only a doorway with a hatch in the wall alongside, beneath a very ornate Georgian canopy. Blackboards were affixed to the walls alongside the openings. Frank Davis, or whoever was stationed there on that particular morning, would laboriously write all the forthcoming tours for the next couple of days on these boards with a 'whitening brush'. Advertising literature would be handed to all passers-by. The boards would be rubbed out daily to accommodate another day's attractions. Wessex, without a doubt, operated the most extensive tours programme of any company in Bristol, if not the entire South West. Empress Coaches had a booking office also in Colston Avenue, and about six doors along from ours. Bristol Tramways were on the opposite side of Colston Street as well, and advertised the full list of Wessex tours as their own in the latter years. All tours started from Anchor Road, about five minutes' walk away from this office.

Wessex *c.* 1956. *Left to right:* Frank Davis, Raymond Jones and Harry Lewis in the doorway of Colston Avenue booking office. That's about all that there was – a hole in the wall beneath an office block, with public toilets across the road.

A large number of drivers were kept on throughout the year. There was plenty of work year-round to keep a high percentage fully employed as drivers. There were still a number of drivers that could turn their hands to other duties such as vehicle painting, coach cleaning, office painting etc., during the winter. They would then be called upon to drive when required, i.e. to cover afternoon school contracts, workers contracts and weekend private hires and tours. Bear in mind that in the '50s, and '60s, as many as 60% of the fleet would be de-licensed and laid up from October to March, so we therefore did not need that many full-time drivers in the winter months anyway. There was a hard-core of seasonal drivers who came back every year, and were as highly thought of as the regulars. Some of these had been seasonally employed for years. These men would go off driving oil tankers, etc. during the winter months, and return some time after Easter. And then there were the numerous part-timers who only came in as needed at weekends and Bank holidays. Each of these categories of driver would have been equally well thought of, and treated the same as a regular driver. After all, some of these had been working weekends only for a considerable length of time – years in some cases.

One name to mention as a part timer would be that of John James. I introduced him to Wessex in 1963. John was the supervisor at the bodyworks that did the 'quietening' work on the ex-Feltham vehicles. He asked me if we ever needed part-timers at weekends, and I brought him in. His wife still blames me for his addiction to coach driving over a period of thirty-eight years. He had already obtained his licence after completing his apprenticeship as a bodybuilder and painter at Bristol Tramways Central Repair works. John continued well after the time of National Express, and finally gave up his badge in year 2000 when he retired. John was a very good servant to Wessex. Gordon Rogers was another long service part-timer who originated with Feltham's. Both went on to do work for Wessex National, as did others too numerous to mention.

Stan Savage was the Private Hire manager at Clifton. He always did the routing and handled the arrangements for Private Hires etc. This usually would involve the booking of meals, arrangements with a pub-stop en route and hotel or theatre bookings where appropriate. The route and instructions would always be specified on the driver's worksheet previously prepared by Stan. The strange thing for a man in this position was that he could not drive – at all. Stan could only prepare a route by looking at a map, and one driver reckoned that he had to be rescued from the middle of the North Sea one day through following Stan's route. We handled our own private-hire work at Kingswood, but all other, or any complicated bookings, would go through Stan's office.

The routes for the excursions and tours were laid down by the Traffic Commissioners and drivers were only supposed to use standard licensed routes, but the older drivers each had their own favourite detours. I remember that some drivers (myself included) used to use the unclassified road over Giants Head between Sherborne and Dorchester to get to Weymouth, but they were not supposed to as there was not a public 'phone for sixteen miles if they broke down. It is still the best road from Bristol to Weymouth. The official route was via Yeovil, but instead we stopped at The Brittania in Castle Cary. This was OK when on 'period bookings' to Weymouth, but if you used this road on an 'advertised tour', you had to return by the other road to show the Cerne Abbas Giant.

While talking of Private Hire, it must be mentioned that a high percentage of year-round work came from this source. We could have in excess of twenty coaches hired by different departments of Bristol University on any Saturday throughout their working year. University Rag Week would need every available coach in March. Winter football trips to away games of the two major Bristol teams had large followings in those days, and Wessex provided the transport for both. The largest hire of the year – every year – took place in May and lasted for three weeks. John James (no, not the aforementioned) the founder of Broadmead Wireless chain had a daughter, Dawn, who was killed in a motor accident when in her teens. John James set up a trust in Dawn's name and, with money generated, became a huge benefactor to the City of Bristol. In May of every year, the Dawn James Trust would take every single pensioner in Bristol on a trip to the seaside, and we would provide the transport five days a week for three weeks. This hire needed over 100 coaches a day and went off to several different locations. We hired everything that Bristol Omnibus could spare, and even brought vehicles in from Black & White at Cheltenham. Not only did the Trust pay for these trips, but it also provided lunch for everyone. I remember that nights out at The Bristol Hippodrome were also included (for which we provided the transport again). The photographs that I show below shows part of the hire outside the Winter Gardens at Bournemouth in 1961, where the passengers appear to have had lunch. Ken Dodd and Alma Cogan were appearing that summer.

There were two shift foremen at Clifton Road garage. Les Jay, whose name I have already mentioned, and George Bascombe ('Bashem'). Les came from Morning Star where he had been a driver for some years, and George from Clifton Greys – his only employer, as he started from school. Each had a team of about four fitters during the season, although the busy period would obviously be late at night when coaches were coming in. No one really knew what time they would be finishing on the late shift. Bert Shapcott ('Shappy') was a long standing ex-driver who went on to the fitting side. Frank Marsh, yet another old-timer, was the electrician. All heavy maintenance work was done at Clifton Road garage. This was the old Maple Leaf headquarters prior to 1947. On the late shift, before about nine o'clock most of the fitters could be found in The Lansdowne, a popular pub opposite the garage. The older drivers always used to ring there first if they had a problem at night, because they knew that they had more chance of finding a fitter in the pub than in the garage. Around about 1966 a fleet engineer by the name of Sid Morrell joined the company. He was a very experienced man who had previously held a similar position for Salopia, a well known Shropshire based touring company of the time. I imagine that he was brought in to cover Bill Jones' pending retirement and, indeed, that of George Bascombe and Les Jay.

Bill Jay, Greg Gregory and Norman Sykes are the drivers.

Seven vehicles reloading after tea and a show at Bournmouth Winter Gardens in 1961.

As already said, the new coaches went to the senior tour drivers – and they were characters themselves. Charlie Bowden was an ex-Scots Guardsman, and he did the Scottish seven-day tour for many years. Charlie was an ex-Clifton Greys driver. He had worked for the Greys for years, going back to their taxi days, and kept his large taxi driver's badge that was earlier required. This badge was as big as a saucer, and for that reason he was sometimes known as 'frying pan Charlie'. When driving he would curse and swear at every other driver on the road, but the passengers used to come back year after year – they loved him, but he was some 'Prima Donna'. He told me one day that he thought that he was the only driver on the company that was worth his salt. He used to stop at Gretna Green going up to Scotland and change into his kilt, which he would then wear for the duration of the tour.

Fred Butler used to do the Norfolk Broads tour. Fred was a very quiet and reserved man and had, for some years previous, worked for Henry Russets Royal Blue Coaches of Bath Road in Bristol. This concern was a haulage and coach operating company, and was therefore nationalised in 1947. The lorries passed to the RHE (British Road Services), and the coaches to Bristol Greyhound. Fred chose to work for Wessex. Bert Hook did the North Wales tour, super chap – suffered badly with asthma. He came from Maple Leaf. Bert Foote did the three-day Cornish tour. Bert Foote was a great pianist and used to entertain the crowd in the overnight hotel stops. Bert was also the union shop steward. Bill Jay (Les Jay's brother) did the Norfolk Broads. Both Bert Foote and Bill Jay were extroverts and could keep the passengers in fits of laughter.

Norman Sykes did the late-season Blackpool weekenders. He and Paddy Boyland were in Weymouth one day, dressed in their obligatory white coats, and spent some time selling deck chairs until they were discovered and chased through the town. One driver, who must remain anonymous, used to come up from Plymouth in April every year and work the season. He was a ladies' man, and had girlfriends everywhere plus a wife in Plymouth. In September, when he finished for the season, he had to be smuggled out in the boot of a coach because there were women waiting for him at every garage exit.

Until 1961 Wessex did not hold any licenses for Saturday 'Period Bookings', but inherited a full package of such from Feltham's. These were operated on summer Saturdays over a thirteen-week period, to Brighton, Bournemouth, Dawlish, Teignmouth, Torquay & Paignton, Seaton, Sidmouth & Exmouth, and Weymouth from their base at Kingswood. As many as thirty coaches could be used at the peak taking people down one week and bringing them back the next. All of these started from our yard in Moravian Rd. (and down the side streets). As can be imagined up to 1200 people at any one time could be milling around our garages (with only one toilet!!!). Now this was manageable if the weather was good but if wet, oh dear, we had problems. The garages would be emptied; any contract deckers parked away would be moved out and parked down the road somewhere. Raymond and I would somehow sort out the chaos and direct the passengers to their respective coaches and at 8.30am all would depart – 2pm at Cheltenham had nothing on it! I can only remember one serious problem, when a loaded coach tried to swing completely around in the back garage and finished up with one wheel down an open pit.

The Kingswood drivers that I was most involved with were also a very good crowd. The core of the drivers was from Feltham's when that company was taken over in 1961. There were characters like Bill Liddington, the fitter, and the driver George Bateman. George was a hard man for the brakes – his brake lights were on more than off if you were following him. He got most annoyed with me one day when I pulled his leg about this. If he came in on the night shift, checked the duty sheet for tomorrow and found that he was on Looe or Aberystwyth, he would defect his brakes. These were the two hardest day tours. On his return the following night the fitters knew that, even if they had done a major job the night before, they would have to do another tonight. Also Stan Peacock, who always went into the paint shop for the winter. Stan was a loner. He did not like running with anyone else – but he could always be relied upon to get the job done. In five years he only crossed me once, and that was on a Saturday night at about 5.30pm.

I was looking forward to an early finish and taking my wife out. Stan was returning from a 'Period' Southsea. He called from the West End (a long-gone hostelry) at Botley, near Southampton, to say that he had a clutch operating rod 'gone'. These shafts were about a metre long and had a habit of snapping or bending, resulting in 'no clutch'. Stan had worked for Pickford's during the war driving heavy haulage, so he must have been used to the old methods of driving without the use of a clutch. I told him to bring it home without the clutch, but he said that he could not do this. I had no drivers: Raymond was away, which left me alone, and I could not get hold of a fitter from Clifton. I had to lock up early and go down to Southampton with another coach. The passengers were not at all happy with Stan having spent nearly four hours waiting and then to find that it was possible to drive it after all.

Both George and Stan appear in the 1946 picture earlier in this article, so they had been with Feltham's for at least fifteen years prior to the takeover of the business. Ken Monks. Ken had such a broad local dialect that some people could not understand what he was saying – especially after a few beers – but he was a much-requested driver for Private Hire work. Frank Corkell. Now, Frank was the sort of chap that everything happened to. Nowadays he can be compared to 'Blakey' in *On the Buses*. He had the cleanest coach in the garage. He was not exactly miserable, but seldom saw the funny side of any situation. Gwen Wilmot, the office person who had also been with Feltham's for some years, used to tell us stories about Frank. Every Monday we would have a catalogue of events of what had happened to him over the weekend. He came in one week, usual long face and we thought: 'Well, what's happened now?' 'Oh it always happens to me, I've had it all now', he moaned. It turns out that he was returning from an advertised tour to Weymouth on the Sunday night, stopped at the Mildmay Arms in Queen Camel and everyone got off except the rather large lady in the back seat. To cut a long story short, she had died and the ambulance crew had considerable difficulty in removing her.

Then there was Terry Brothers. Terry could not get up in the morning. Terry's coach was always spotless – he could not be faulted in this respect. He also had a pleasant and polite way of handling the passengers, and was much requested for private hire jobs, but if he was due to come in at 6am and be out at 7 he would show up at about 6.55am, by which time I had his duty covered by someone else. His argument was, quite rightly, that he had cleaned his coach the night before when he came in, but I could not afford to wait until he was due out and then find that he had not turned up, so I started covering his duty and he became 'spare' to take the place of the next man who did not turn up. He and I had massive arguments over this, causing him to complain to Raymond and the union that I was victimising him, but he did not get much change from either because Raymond had suffered the same problem with him when he was on earlies. I think that I cured him, though, and we got on well after that. Terry left in the end and went to work for Warner's (of Tewkesbury) who had taken over the Co-op fleet in Bristol. We had given a continental private hire job to Terry and I think that he must have got the taste because Warner's at that time were starting to do continental work and that is what he went for.

Harry Cridland was an ex-publican. We put Harry through for his licence; he was a very large, jolly man, over twenty-three stone in weight, and he had to have his seat so far back to accommodate his stomach that he was almost sat on the front passenger seat behind him. He was on the Yate workers run one evening, with an almost equally large lady who used to sit in the front seat behind the driver every night to return to Frampton Cottrell. This night she must have had trouble standing up, so she leant forward and grabbed the back of Harry's seat to help her and pulled the seat completely off its fixings. Harry apparently hung on and stopped the coach but then turned around and called Mabel a lot of words that we couldn't find in the dictionary. Then there was 'Wilfy' Guest. Every company has one – and he was ours. Never ever saw the serious side of anything; life was one long laugh to him. He was close to retirement, and only worked Mondays to Fridays on contract work unless we were desperate and could fit him into a contract or schools job on a Saturday. Wilfy had bad eyesight. Worse than that, he had glasses like pebbles. He said to me one day that if ever Bedford OBs came back into fashion he would have to pack up driving because he would not be able to see beyond the radiator filler cap. I *think* that he was only joking …

In the winter we would have maybe six or eight coaches a day on schools and workers terminating at Yate. We would therefore leave all but one coach parked in Yate, and the drivers would return to the garage in one vehicle and go back to Yate at 3pm. I was usually among the afternoon crowd if one of the regulars was on another job. On the return journey we would all visit 'Mr Lane's Café' for a cup of tea and a piece of his home made lardy cake. On the way out to Yate, all in the one coach, we would have driving competitions. A glass of water would be placed on the step and on a daily basis we would see who could drive the furthest without spilling the water. As I have said, during the winter at least 60% of the fleet was delicensed in those days and vehicles were stored in our (Kingswood) 'back garage'. Our drivers at Kingswood would get so bored that they used to bring the vehicles out, clean them and park them up again, just to keep occupied. We had to keep these drivers employed because we had extensive school and works contracts morning and evening, and at weekends we sometimes needed to bring in part-timers to cover the private hire and football trip commitments.

As you may imagine, we had all sorts of drivers applying for jobs at the start of a season. Some came to us from Bristol Omnibus and had never been outside of the Bristol boundaries; some had been lorry drivers and thought that they would have a change; some came to us without licences and according to the quality of the individual, *and* how hard up we were for drivers, we would put them through their test. From about 1965 onward I would take an applicant out for assessment, give him some tuition and then pass him on to George Bascombe to put him through his test. One ex-lorry driver stands out in my memory. We took on a man who previously had obtained his badge with the bus company, but had latterly spent a couple of years driving for Kleeneze brushes, a company that was based locally. Now Kleeneze drivers used to go away on a Sunday with about 400 home deliveries all over the UK in a seven-ton van, and get home on the following Friday or Saturday. I was told that they were driving flat-out all the time to get their deliveries covered. One Sunday – this chap must have been on afternoon tour – he had done his pick-ups and was on his way into town but he called at the office on his way through. I was standing in the glass-fronted office as he drove up Moravian Road rather fast and pulled up outside of the office. As he stopped, he braked so hard that forty-one bums came up off their seats and went back down again. I had to call him into the office to lecture him and to point out that he was now carrying people and not sweeping brushes.

During the winter as many drivers as possible were found work. There was general vehicle maintenance to be carried out, and vehicle certification was always arranged for the off-season period when drivers would help with the presentation of vehicles. There were no steam-cleaners or pressure-washers as there are today. Part of the job entailed putting the front wheels up onto a concrete ramp, spraying the underside of the coach with a cold-water pressure hose (in the dead of winter) cleaning, and then painting the underside with silver paint. This was a Ministry requirement. Some examiners were flexible and tolerant, they knew and appreciated the work that went into a pre-certification overhaul, but others were not. When a coach was new it came with a seven-year 'certificate of fitness', but on its expiry this work had to be done. The coach would be thoroughly overhauled from front to back and top to bottom. Seats were removed and rebuilt, floor coverings would be replaced, complete floors replaced if necessary, head linings were cleaned and the vehicle repainted. All mechanical units were checked and overhauled where necessary. If the inspection was successful it was given a five-year 'ticket' but maybe two, three or four if the standard of overhaul was not good. At twelve years old the process began again.

George Bascombe once boasted to me that he had never had a failure – all went through first and second time for the full five years. One year, it must have been 1966, the twelve SAEs were being put through. A new examiner checked everything and could find nothing wrong with one particular vehicle until he opened the rear boot doors. The boot interior had been painted silver and newspaper had been placed over the new paint for protection. 'Get that out of there before I see this vehicle again' said the examiner as he slammed the doors shut – and failed it. Coaches still received interim inspections every twelve months, as now, and if a vehicle had been involved in an accident, it had to be inspected before any work was carried out – exactly as now. There were drivers who were good at repairing seats and interior trim; some came in and did interior decorating to the offices. Agents' advertising boards had to be made, repaired or repainted so the winter was a busy time for all. Me, I spent my first two winters catching up on the Ministry passenger returns that had been somewhat neglected previously.

There was an in house body shop at Clifton Road. No coach was allowed to be seen on the road with dents and scrapes on it. All damaged vehicles went straight into the body shop for attention from Ken Walters and his team. When the coaches came out of there, they went to the paint shop at Lawrence Hill where another team of drivers worked. In 1959 the exterior paint scheme of the coaches was reversed, resulting in all vehicles having a complete repaint. Yes there was plenty of work to be done on top of the private hire work and football and rugby trips, which would happen at weekends.

Somewhere to the rear of Whiteladies Road offices was a rented property that was used as the trim shop. Len Windmill used to work here as an upholsterer/ seat trimmer, but also carried out interior repairs to coaches. Len had previously worked for Bristol Cars fitting out the luxury models and later came to Wessex. Whether he was self-employed or employed I never knew.

At Kingswood we had our own fitter who would do the minor jobs on a day-to-day basis. Bill Liddington was also in his sixties and had been with Feltham's since the day dot, as had his late father for some years before him. I think that he resented Wessex, because Feltham's were a much smaller company and they treated him as one of the family. Come the takeover and his work was somewhat diluted. Bill and I always seemed to cross swords – he did not like taking instructions from me at all. Bill was a 'dirty' fitter. His boots would be thick with grease and oil from the workshop floor, but he would insist in coming into the office for his morning and afternoon tea, as he had done for years, and would walk straight through everywhere, leaving oily footmarks across our clean tiled floor. In the end we banned him from the office – that did not go down very well.

Once a year, in September, I did the Southend Illuminations tour. One year I spent all day on the Friday cleaning the coach until it was immaculate – I always liked a spotless coach. I had to use it to cover a workers return from Yate late on the Friday afternoon, and whilst coming in I noticed that the oil pressure light was flashing as I drove. I knew that a Bedford 300 had an oil pressure switch with a 4lb breaking pressure, so I told Bill and he said that he would look at it that evening. I went home, coming in at 6am next morning knowing that my coach was spotlessly clean, only to find that Bill had walked up and down the gangway to the back of the coach (for whatever reason) with his greasy boots and left his footprints all the way. To say that I was annoyed would be putting it mildly, and we had a blazing row early that morning. I did my Southend, getting back at 6am Sunday morning. On Monday I said to Bill, 'The light didn't come on Bill, what did you do put a new switch in'. 'No', he said, 'I took the bulb out.' That was another few words that he and I had. Bill and I invariably used to do the Saturday and Sunday night 'Mystery Tour', simply because no one else wanted to. This mystery tour was a bit of a tradition with Feltham's, and we inherited it. They had operated it for years and, before my time, Bill and Albert Feltham had covered it. The same regulars used to go week after week all through the season. I think that the fare was 4/6d. If another driver did happen to do the trip and went the wrong way or did it differently, there would be ructions amongst the regular passengers. We had several different routes and it was up to us where we went really, but you had to drive for thirty minutes, stop at a pub for about thirty minutes, and then drive for another thirty minutes, by which time you invariably had to be in either Chipping Sodbury or Clevedon for another drink and Fish & Chips. Then home by 9.30pm.

For very many years Wessex carried Bristol City FC, Bristol Rovers FC and Bristol Rugby Club. All of the public schools in Bristol used Wessex. Contracts were ongoing with Bristol Education Committee as well as Gloucestershire County Council. During the winter I was kept busy with the booking agents' needs and visiting schools for the procurement of private hire trips. I also did more driving in the winter than I did in the summer. If the Bristol football teams were doing well we could have over forty coaches at a time on the supporters' trips. It had been known for de-licensed vehicles to be put back on the road for one weekend, or even 1 day in the case of evening matches. This, of course, meant taxing them for a complete month. Bristol City played Blackpool in the cup one year and we were all out on that one. It was an evening kick-off (perhaps a replay).

Terry Brothers was returning with one of the split screen Super Vegas when a stone smashed the nearside screen. At that time, before the M6, and as on the returning Blackpool illuminations trips in the autumn, we used to pull into the Potteries (PMT) depot at Stoke on Trent in the early hours of the morning and use their canteen for refreshments. So the driver 'phoned from there, got young George out of bed at 2am and told him the situation. George said, 'Well, so what?' The driver said 'I am in Stoke, can we borrow a Potteries' vehicle to get home? They are complaining of the cold.' It must have been -5°C at least. George said, 'No. Tell them to put their overcoats on.' So, home he came. Such was the philosophy of hired vehicles.

One personality who deserves a mention here was not even employed by Wessex but by Dunlop Rubber Co. All tyres that the vehicles were running on were leased from Dunlop's at so much a mile each. Jack Hodge was permanently based at Clifton Road or Kingswood garage to deal with any problems, and every day he had to note the odometer reading of each vehicle. Jack had only one good arm. The other had been amputated at the elbow but he could change a wheel and tyre as easily and quickly as any two-armed fitter. I don't know whether Jack had any home to go to but, as far as I can remember, he was at the garage early in the morning and still there late at night after coaches had come back in, checking the tyres of every single vehicle. People probably said that about all the operational staff anyway. I always used to say that we started work at about 5.30am on Good Friday and worked right through until the afternoon tours had left on the first Sunday in October. Les Jay always used to say 'We are like 'The Windmill', we never close.' For the younger readers, The Windmill was a theatre in London that opened twenty-four hours a day – even during the blitz.

After I had been employed for about three years Raymond and I came to an agreement that we would each have one Sunday off in three. I worked a full Sunday this week, half a day next week, alternating between morning and afternoon and the third Sunday I had off. Raymond worked to the reverse pattern to ensure that the office was always covered. I also used to finish at lunchtime on a Tuesday. On this time off I would go out driving to earn extra money. I was allowed to take my wife on tours with me if there was a vacant seat on the coach. The hours were long in the summer, but we tried to make up for this in the winter. Having said that, if a Private Hire was leaving at 3am in the winter, either Raymond or I had to be there to make sure that the driver had in fact turned up. This actually happened one Boxing Day morning. Bear in mind that holidays for everyone could only be taken off-season, between October and March, and even then it was on a first come first served basis to ensure that we had adequate numbers of staff available.

The other names of senior drivers that come to mind would be Bill Ruck, Tommy Taylor, 'Ginger' Hallett, George Stephens, Charlie Murray, Reg Toop, Bert Crane, Larry Seamer, Bert Shapcott (fitter/driver), Norman Sykes, Greg Gregory, Geoff. Jenkins, and, before my time but still spoken highly of, Freddie Horst, 'Smudger' Smith, Fred Harper, Maurice Lawrence, Lou Crane, Lionel Dudbridge, Stan Bellamy, and many more to whom I express my apologies for omitting their names.

Alas, at the time of writing all these characters are only names– with the exception of 'young' George, Raymond and myself.

An advertising board as supplied to all booking agents. This particular example now resides on the wall of the premises of Bristol Vintage Bus Group at Brislington, Bristol.

Wessex Coaches Ltd.
Phone 34001   **BRISTOL**
(Incorporating "CLIFTON GREYS" "MORNING STAR" & "MAPLE LEAF" Services)

Tour to ....

Date ....   Seat No. ....

Cash Paid ....   Signed ....
                                             Booking Agent.

Start from ....   Time............ Coach............

Ticket No. **G 20399**

The Company reserve the right to cancel this booking at any time, if, in the Company's opinion, circumstances render such cancellation necessary or desirable.

Wessex Coaches Ltd.
Phone 34001   **BRISTOL**
(Incorporating "CLIFTON GREYS" "MORNING STAR" & "MAPLE LEAF" Services)

Tour to ....

Date ....   Seat No. ....

Cash Paid ....   Signed ....
                                             Booking Agent.

Start from ....   Time............ Coach............

Ticket No. **G 20400**

The Company reserve the right to cancel this booking at any time, if, in the Company's opinion, circumstances render such cancellation necessary or desirable.

Book a ticket to Weston – or anywhere else for that matter – and you would be given one of these, and that did not change for the life of the company.

CHAPTER 11

The Remuneration and Conditions

Drivers have never been among the better-paid section of the community, whether they drive coaches or lorries. In the postbag each Thursday morning I would receive the payslips for each of the employed Kingswood drivers, together with a cheque equating to the total amount involved. I would then have to go to the Bank, cash the cheque and make up the weekly pay packets. From the petty cash, I would also make up the wages for the part-timers. Wessex was a fully trade union closed shop. Union membership was sometimes necessary to gain entry into the Bristol Bus Station or Victoria, although I was never a member, being a salaried staff employee, and was never challenged. Because of the presence of the TGWU, pay structures were laid down by agreement and strictly governed. In 1963 I know that a driver was paid a basic guaranteed wage of £9 15s 0d for a 45-hour week spread over five days (any five in six excluding Sunday) and a rate of payment for overtime which I cannot remember.

I know that it was a most peculiar formula needed to calculate a total. The driver was paid overtime rate for all hours in excess of the first forty-five commencing on Monday at 2am. Saturday would be classed as the fifth working day if he had had a day off in the week, otherwise it was treated as the sixth day at overtime rate. Sunday would be overtime paid at a further enhanced rate but, again, I cannot remember what. The driver's pay had to be supplemented with his tips, on which he was totally dependent; therefore, the drivers who got the best jobs earned the most money, the driver who took the trouble to look after his passengers did better at the end of the day. Drivers' earnings would drop later in the season, tailing off to basic wages in the winter if things were quiet, and then increase over Easter to drop again until mid-May. He did not have to have a rest day at any time and could be used by the company for seven days a week when it suited them. The law only specified that he had to have so many hours rest in 24 and that his 24 hour period commenced at 2am. It was left to the traffic office to allot the work so that the driver could catch up on his sleep. Thus if he did a long day to Looe, Aberystwyth or maybe Brighton today, starting at 6am and finishing at about 11pm, we would make sure that tomorrow he either came in at 12 noon for an afternoon tour or he could do a Weymouth or Bournemouth starting at 6.45am and finishing at about 9.30pm, giving him about 5 hours to rest (on the back seat) during the day. Drivers fully accepted this, as they knew it was the only way that they were likely to earn a 'decent' week's wage.

This made our job in the traffic office rather difficult, as we had to be seen to be fair with the work schedules, whilst trying to keep within the drivers' hours' laws that did exist. These were not as strictly enforced on PSV drivers as they were on HGV drivers. PSV drivers did not keep a daily log sheet at that time. With this in mind, we had to ensure that work was evened out across the board, otherwise drivers would be in the office complaining that 'He's had more hours than me!' If I remember correctly, part-timers were paid three shillings an hour Monday to Saturday, and four shillings on Sundays. This created further problems. Because of the trade union involvement, we had to be very sure that we did not favour a part-timer and give him a better job than a regular driver. There were occasions when one knew that the available part-timer was much more worthy of the job in hand than the scruffy individual that one employed last week to cover contracts, so one somehow had to juggle the work around to ensure that the employed man was given no reason to complain. There were further complications involving me personally. Again, because of the union agreement, I could not go out driving if there was a driver on the sheet on 'day off', unless he had requested that day off, because I was a 'staff driver'. I could not be seen to be doing a 'better' job than a driver covering, shall we say, afternoon schools and workers, unless the job had arisen because of unforeseen circumstances. Drivers could request a day off, but would have to have a very good reason for the request to be granted if we were busy.

It was sometimes more difficult in the winter to keep everyone happy. Maybe it was a quiet week; we had only contracts to cover. When preparing the duty sheet one would decide that there were too many drivers tomorrow, so, say, four drivers have to be given a day off. I, (preparing the duty sheet) on, Tuesday, for example, would think to myself, 'We are going to need three drivers in on Saturday for the football trips, so I can make up five hours of their time there – I know, I'll bring this one in at 12.00 'spare' tomorrow. He is now be going to work five hours, probably kicking his heels and be paid five hours to cover maybe two hours' work on Saturday. Five hours was a minimum day. Between the two, he has gained an hour over his guaranteed nine-hour day, and worked his forty-five hours, plus the hour at overtime rate.' The fourth driver's time would be left to juggle another day.

This was another disadvantage to the driver: he really had no say as to when he was to have a day off next week – it was purely based on the company workload for the following day. Further, he would not be aware that he had a day off tomorrow until he finished work today and checks the duty sheet were posted up in the garage at about 5pm. If he had requested a day off and being winter-time it was granted, he was now reduced to a four-day week, and only had to be paid for thirty-six hours. A very complicated system and totally unbalanced against the driver, but I think that was how it worked. It was a common occurrence to have drivers come into the office complaining about work allocation, and the traffic department had to be seen to be scrupulously fair in allocating the work daily and to have an answer to such a complaint.

Drivers, of course, had their own pet methods of earning a few bob extra. For instance, refreshment stops always gave the driver a cup of tea and maybe a sandwich with no charge; some cafés would give him a small cash sum on top of this, (usually 2s 6d). Those stops that did not tip the driver found that coaches did not stop at their restaurant any more, and word soon got around

Harry Lewis at his retirement party.

about where the best places were. I personally recall the old lady at Symonds Yat, Rose Cottage. This lady opened up her garden and conservatory to visitors in the summer months, and provided teas and refreshments for the coach parties. She always gave the driver 2*s* 6*d* and a boiled egg sandwich, never anything different – always a boiled egg sandwich. Longleat house was always good for 2*s* 6*d* and a free tea in the days before The Safari Park, when we used to park at the side of the house. This was a super afternoon tour and included Heavens Gate and Shearwater. The show of rhododendrons was fabulous, but they also used to stage afternoon 'pop' concerts, which always attracted large crowds. A driver would recommend certain restaurants when visiting a resort such as Weymouth, Looe or Ilfracombe and then pay his visit for a free lunch or whatever later.

Looe! Now that was a money-spinning trip, although I can swear that I never did this because I never actually did the tour. When the Tamar Bridge was newly opened in the early 1960s, the toll for a coach to cross was 1*s* 6*d*. The Looe tour was routed via Okehampton, Tavistock and Liskeard. The return same route, but when about to leave Looe, the driver would say to the passengers, 'Tell you what, I'm not supposed to, but for an extra 6*d* a head to cover the bridge toll, I will take you back via Plymouth so that you can see the new bridge'. Everybody fell for it and he would pocket the 18*s* 6*d* difference. Sometime after I left, the route was changed to include Plymouth – so that put an end to that little 'fiddle'. There were other ways for the driver to earn a few bob extra to which I was not always privy, but I was told very early on in my career that, when returning from a tour, always get out of one's seat to open the door and help passengers down the steps. It was an act of courtesy that a passenger would expect, but it was amazing that some drivers did not bother to do so. When stood at the bottom of the steps, one helped people out and was ready to accept a 'tip' from the satisfied passenger – always, after the first passenger, with half-a-crown in the hand so that the next one (hopefully) felt obliged to give that much also. It used to work a treat.

CHAPTER 12

The Properties

Wessex Coaches Ltd worked from several different offices and properties. Most of these were owned by the company and were very valuable and prestigious assets. I will list the addresses from which the company was operated.

1   71/73 Whiteladies Road, Clifton, Bristol. Both came with the Clifton Greys business, making a very valuable detached property. This was the registered office of the company. The upper rooms had been converted into flats, and one of these was occupied by Mr Bellamy. Behind and below this property, fronting onto Hampton Lane, was a small workshop that in the fifties or sixties would hold, possibly, two to three coaches. This was where vehicles were brought for their interiors to be cleaned, and to carry out any upholstery repairs. I believe that this lower floor was later converted to office use. There was a converted shop premises in Aberdeen Road and backing on to Hampton Lane where Len Windmill, the upholsterer, worked.

2   Clifton Road Garage, Clifton. The premises was formerly occupied by Maple Leaf Coaches (C.W. Jordan) and again, a very valuable asset of the company (although it was leased). This had capacity for about twenty-five vehicles with four pits. This site has since been developed with a block of luxury flats. There was an annexe to this garage fronting onto Lansdown Road, holding about eight coaches. This was always referred to as 'the Ministry'. It was possible for 38-seaters to reverse in, off Lansdown Road, but otherwise it was used for the 'half-cab' 35-seaters. Modern coaches would not have got in.

3   Colston Avenue Booking Office, the Tramways Centre. Inherited from Maple Leaf, who had used it for many years as their booking office, this office occupied a prime spot on the Centre which was then the focal point for visitors to the city and West Country.

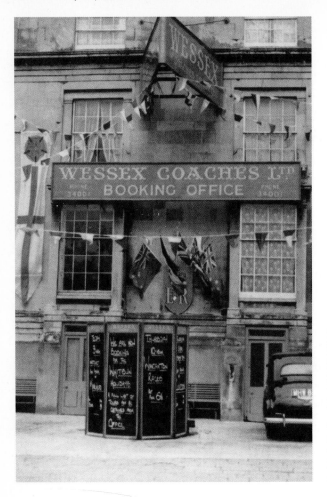

71 Whiteladies Road, decorated
for the coronation in 1952.
Below: c. 1936. Colston Avenue
Booking Office is seen on the
bottom right hand side while still
operated by Maple Leaf Coaches.
Trams are still in operation
and a Greyhound coach awaits
departure time on the left. The
van in the foreground is a Royal
Mail Morris Commercial of
15cwt capacity.

4   17 Lawrence Hill was a Morning Star property. It was used as a booking office and about 200 yards away from the original Morning Star garage premises.

5   Wellington Street, Lawrence Hill. Formerly used a garage by Morning Star, this was a building capable of holding about four or five coaches and was latterly used as the paint shop.

6   54 Moravian Road, Kingswood, Bristol. Purchased with the business of G.F. Feltham & Sons Ltd (Kingswood Queen). On this site Feltham's built a bungalow to house the offices in 1956, and Wessex extended this for Raymond and his family to live in the upstairs flat in 1961. On this site was a very large hard-surfaced yard on which probably fifty or sixty coaches could have parked in the open. At the rear of the yard was an ex-wartime hangar-type building which still survives today as a woodworking workshop. This garage could hold probably a further forty coaches. To the front of the yard was another garage/workshop with pit facilities and holding for another nine coaches. Fuel bunkering facilities were on the site. This property was sold in its entirety to National Bus Company.

7   There were office premises in Fore Street, Chard.

8   At Furnham Road, Chard, was a large open yard, at some time the site of a US army base, where the coaches and early contract vehicles were located. This site became the Furzehill council estate.

9   I believe that there were booking offices in Bridport and Lyme Regis.

10   What could have really been the icing on the cake was a huge piece of land at Lawrence Hill, next door to the Bunch of Grapes public house. This ground was open and undeveloped, and I recall seeing the plans for a very large Bus Station to serve the whole of Bristol as well as providing a central garage for the whole fleet. Mr G.J. Jones (who personally owned the site) submitted these plans and they were refused. One can see why now. The site has been buried forever under Lawrence Hill roundabout, a major junction on the inner city ring road. This was a major pick-up point for Wessex on the way into town, it being only 100 yards from the old Morning Star booking office and premises. A lot of trade was still drawn from the area. We used to pick up passengers on the road just out of the picture below. To save valuable time on pick-ups, the drivers did not like to make the detour around to the rear of the site, apart from which the site was covered in rubble and not really good for passengers to have to walk through. Every so often, the Police would stop coaches loading on the road and force drivers to go around the back and to enter via Catherine Street.

All tours started from Anchor Road, later moved to the old goods yard in Canons Marsh, and where the modern development occupied by Millennium Square now stands, but in Anchor Road, was a small Nissan hut situated at about where the access road to Cathedral Square is now situated. In this hut was nothing but a telephone mounted on a pole but it enabled staff to keep in touch with Whiteladies Road or Kingswood should there be any problems. As I remember Bert Fielding of Empress also had a key to the hut so the 'phone was for his use also. This building could hardly be called a property.

All of these properties came to the group from the companies involved in the formation. I have listed the properties as I remember them. After all these years, my memory does not always stand the test; if there are more I stand to be corrected. Regarding the vehicle capacities quoted in the case of the garages, I am again speaking from memory, and about vehicles somewhat smaller than those produced today.

The gateway on the right led to a rubble strewn bomb-site entered from Catherine Street at the rear ...

... and what lay behind those hoardings at Lawrence Hill!

CHAPTER 13

The Local Competition

As I have previously said, during the 1950s and on into the '60s, not many people owned cars. The demand for coach travel was at its peak. Wessex Coaches Ltd offered a range of day tours, afternoon tours and evening tours that, it is fair to say, no other Bristol operator could match. If I remember rightly, only Wessex, and maybe Bristol Greyhound, was licensed to pick up passengers all over Bristol. To cover the range of tours offered, the company picked up passengers in every single district and suburb of the city and surrounds. Local licensed operators also had pick-ups from within their local areas, and maybe Empress, Monarch and Bristol Co-op had more coverage than most, but none had the extended coverage of Wessex and Bristol Greyhound. From Kingswood we also provided coverage for passengers wishing to travel from Wick, Oldland, Bitton, Pucklechurch, Frenchay, Downend, all districts in South Gloucestershire, as well as covering those pick-ups en route to Anchor Road.

The downside of this coverage was of course the extended times that it took to collect people from these points and, more importantly, to deliver them back after a tour. The actual pick-up time for a person joining at, say, Bitton was fifty-five minutes before the departure time at Anchor Road in the centre of Bristol. Pick-up schedules were arranged as near as possible to enable a direct route to be followed into Bristol, but on the return it was a different story. It must be remembered that a coach on any tour would have had passengers from all over Bristol joining it at Anchor Road and, upon the return, these people had to be taken back to their joining point. Drivers invariably sorted themselves out and would meet in the centre of the city at a given time and swap passengers, so that one driver would deliver to one side and vice versa. Passengers would invariably get upset. Everyone wanted to be the first to get off no matter where he or she had got on. People used to say, 'I was picked up first, I should be dropped off first', but it never worked out that way, these would be the last off.

I recall a return that I once did from Weston one night with a 38-seater, and it took me fifty minutes from Weston Sea Front to the Hen & Chicken at Bedminster, and a further hour and fifty-five minutes from the Hen & Chicken to Longwell Green. A 7pm return such as this would have had no other driver to work with, if there was only one coach on Weston that day. You can appreciate the problem. The reason, incidentally, that I was doing this trip was that at the busy times a coach would take the people to Weston at 10am. That coach and driver would return to Bristol either to cover an afternoon tour at 2.30pm, or maybe to do a schools and workers run or a Private Hire. If the timings were right for either job, then that same driver could go back and do the return Weston afterwards, but if the times did not fall right and the morning driver was otherwise engaged, a staff driver or part-timer would do it at 7pm. I have said that drivers met up on return but sometimes, especially early and late season, there may be no one that he can tie up with and, in that case, some passengers had a long ride home.

Some drivers refused to work together as one or the other had been caught with 'drops', which would have been inconvenient to both parties being offloaded. Most were OK, and it was not in any driver's interest to be otherwise. I personally had a case one night where I met a driver in town, Charlie Murray – he's long gone now – and we swapped passengers. We compared loading charts and decided which passengers we could take from each other. I did all of my drops this night and finished at Downend, but when I got back on the coach there was a little old chap sat all on his own in one of the middle seats. I asked where he was going and he said 'Shirehampton'. I had then to travel about 12 miles across the city to drop him off and another 12 miles plus to return to Kingswood. Bear in mind that it was probably 10pm or later by then. Charlie, as a Clifton driver, could have covered this far easier than me but chose not to do so. Needless to say, I never ever worked this system with Charlie again.

We operated three- five- and seven-day holiday tours – these were always called Extended Tours and later, Land Cruises. The seven-day Scottish tour departed on a Saturday, but the North Wales, Cornwall, Surrey, Sussex & Kent and the five-day Norfolk Broads and Lake District tours left on a Sunday. Nothing but the best hotels and the newest coaches were used on these trips; it would be unusual if any seats were vacant on the departing tours. No other Bristol company offered this type of service. Day/afternoon trips left Bristol at 7.15am, 8am, 8.45am, 10am, and 2.30pm and a few 6.30pm Evening Tours. A full week's tour listing appears elsewhere.

7.15am departures would typically be to Brighton, Looe, or Aberystwyth. 8am departures would typically be to Torquay & Paignton, Southsea, London & Windsor or Swansea and Mumbles (no Severn Bridge before 1966). 8.45am departures would typically be to Weymouth or Bournemouth. 10 am departures would typically be to Weston, Minehead (for Butlins Camp), Stratford on Avon or Salisbury. 2.30pm Departures would typically be to Weston, Minehead (afternoon drive), Cheddar & Weston, Wells, Burnham & Weston, Malvern Hills, Longleat, Cotswolds & Broadway etc. The most popular tour of all was the Sunday afternoon Mystery Tour. This tour did not come into its own until about 1967-8, but was certainly the most popular of the week, with sometimes eight coaches on the one tour alone. Greg Gregory was always on the first coach, and he set the routes for the others so that they did not fall over each other.

With the improvements to the road network and shortening of journey times, particularly of the longer day-trips, the 7.15am departures were retarded to 8am, and the 8ams became 8.30am later. The Sunday afternoon Mystery Tour was the real money-spinner, and was later duplicated with a 10am departure, which became even more popular. As many as ten coaches could be deployed on the morning tour, usually manned by senior drivers with instructions to split up and go anywhere within a set mileage limit of about 150 miles for the day. The same people used to travel week after week and could specify the driver with whom they wanted to travel. The same driver then had to be allotted to coach— every week.

This would be only a very small selection of what was available. As I have said, the choice was endless. Saturdays intentionally tended to be rather quiet for day or half-day tours. Every single vehicle could be away on express service. A half-day trip would be advertised if it could fit in with a returning express service, but things used to change so quickly at the height of the season that it did not always operate to plan. By about 12 noon sometimes heads would be scratched as to where we were going to get a coach from to operate a tour that had been advertised for days. That returning coach that we expected could easily be 'hijacked' at Birmingham or Cheltenham by Associated Motorways and end up in London or just about anywhere. At the very worst, and given a window of about two hours, another coach could be scrambled from Chard – if the so-called 'spare' had been utilised and if there was a coach spare at Chard. If that option failed, we would hand all booked passengers over to Empress and they would operate the tour as theirs. Several Saturday vehicles were engaged in the period bookings traffic, and as many as could be mustered would be on hire to Bristol Tramways for Associated Motorways journeys. Sadly, by the 1970s demand for these types of tours had all but vanished.

Historically there had always been other tour operators in Bristol, all making a living and fighting for the available business – of which there was plenty. Listings in the 1928 edition of Kelly's Directory shows that Maple Leaf had a booking office at 1 Colston Avenue. Maid of the Mountains were at No. 5, Greyhound

Motors at No.7 and Empress Coaches at No. 15. Clifton Greys, Pioneer Motors (S. Russett) and Royal Blue Motors (H. Russett) are also listed as having offices in Colston Avenue, whilst Morning Star's office was situated on the opposite side of the Tramway Centre at 7 Broad Quay. After 1948, Empress Coaches (as mentioned) was probably the largest operator next to Wessex and Bristol Tramways in the city, and retained their city centre booking office with agents around the districts, as Wessex did also. Their tours also started from Anchor Road, and there was always an element of friendly rivalry between Bert Fielding and us. Fielding, who owned Empress, had taken over the licenses of both Imperial Coaches and Monarch Coaches over the years to give greater coverage, but he still did not have as extensive a listing as Wessex. Both Imperial and Monarch had been based at Eastville.

Bristol Tramways *advertised* a daily list of tours also from Anchor Road and pick-ups around the city, using Greyhound vehicles of course, but they were rather spasmodic in their operation due to vehicles being committed to express services. From the late 1960s onwards a copy of the Wessex tours list was printed in exactly the same format as that of Wessex, but in a different colour scheme with Bristol Greyhound's name at the heading, to be distributed to Greyhound booking agents. All bookings made were charted and operated by Wessex, with Bristol Greyhound receiving a percentage of the ticket value.

The Kingswood/Staple Hill area was probably the most contested. The problem was that the local operators such as Renown and Wiltshire's (Princess Mary) collected their clientele from within a small radius of their premises and started their tours locally. All Wessex tours started from Anchor Road in the centre of Bristol but, particularly with the Kingswood office, we also picked people up in the outlying areas and villages. Some people were against the long times that our pick-ups took, and went to other operators. As I have already said, at the extreme, there would be a 55-minute journey from Wick or Bitton to Anchor Road, and the same on the return unless the tour returned in that direction. Passengers picked up at the start of the route would be facing a long ride into town and long journey before their tour commenced. We used to pass it off as a joke, saying that they were getting a free tour of Bristol into the bargain.

Sometimes, particularly when we were quieter, the feeder coach would come into Kingswood depot from, say, Bitton and people would be transferred from that coach to another coming in from say, Downend and Staple Hill and only one would then run into town – a further hassle. Because of the inconvenience some people preferred to go to the competition, but these only ran the most popular trips such as Weston, Weymouth, Bournemouth and Torquay – and then not every day of the week as we did. S.G. Wiltshire (Princess Mary) ran a business with a style close to that of Feltham's and Burchill's, before Wessex took the latter two over. Wiltshire's, Princess Mary Coaches, was a family business run by the old chap

c. 1890. An outing by Wiltshire's brake from Wesleyan Chapel, Soundwell.

Middle and below: Mr Wiltshire appears in both of these photographs. On the left he is stood against the coach in the foreground, and on the right stood in the gateway with DG 7935 emerging from the yard.

Above and below: Two earlier photographs of Princess Mary vehicles.

Right and middle: Two of
the last vehicles purchased
both are now preserved.

A pair of Guy Vixens in
Cliff Davis's garage at
Staple Hill. The vehicle on
the right has been preserved
and is in the Black Country
Museum at Dudley.

himself and drivers the passengers knew. He had a fleet of about eight coaches, which were very tidy and up to date. Mr Wiltshire himself was a Chapel man, and would not run his coaches on a Sunday unless it was a job for the chapel. He drove a coach himself up to the age of 83, keeping an immaculate Bedford OB for this purpose. I recall that it had a Longwell Green body. Sid would not drive the bigger vehicles. Princess Mary Coaches were based at Soundwell. He passed away in 1978 aged 94. Of all the companies and properties mentioned in this article, the yard at Soundwell is the only one that still houses an active coach business today.

An interesting little story of how the name Princess Mary Coaches came about. A member of Sid Wiltshire's family told the story in the Bristol Evening Post in 1994. Princess Mary married Lord Lascelles on the day that he ran his very first motor coach, a solid-tyred Model T Ford. Prior to this, he had been the youngest four-horse team driver in the Bristol area. Princess Mary were, apparently, the first to operate a workers service from the Kingswood area to Filton Aero Works before the war, and I believe that this service ran until the time that the business was sold.

In the midst of a family dispute in 1964, Mr Wiltshire's nephew, Don, parted company with Princess Mary, which continued to be run by Don's brother, Ralph, until being sold to Eagle Coaches of Bristol, a company still operating a very smart fleet today. Don was very well known and liked by the Princess Mary clientele. He bought a second-hand 41-seat Duple-Vega from Renown and did a bit of Private Hire around about 1964-5, but later took over the business and garage of Clifford's Coaches, (Cliff Davies) further down Soundwell Road. Don later purchased a second-hand Bedford Val, which was driven by his daughter, and then replaced the Vega with a new Ford/Plaxton, which retained the colours of silver and blue of his

Leyland TS4 Tiger
C32F FGC 890
belonging to Grews
Coaches (Majestic).

JDG 267 was a 1947 Vulcan with a C29F body which later passed to Sparkes.

first coach as used by Renown. When he retired, this coach, CDG 314K, passed to Sparkes of Warmley. The last I saw of it, the coach was being used as a 'greasy spoon' just off the M4 near Bridgend. I even went in for a bacon sandwich – only for old time's sake. A picture of this vehicle appears with the 'Sparkes' pictures.

Don started doing a few advertised tours for which Cliff had held licenses but rarely operated. Cliff used to operate one vehicle only, a very ancient Guy Vixen, but only really on the school contracts. Burchill's Renown Coaches operated a programme of tours prior to takeover by Wessex in 1965. Crews Coaches (Majestic) operated tours from Staple Hill, 300 yards away from Burchill's garage in Broad Street. For some reason, I never had any contact with Crews which, again, was an old established business that must have kept itself very much to itself. They, as I remember, operated a small fleet of older heavyweight vehicles – Leylands and Albions.

Next there was the Co-op at Fishponds. Bristol Co-operative Society Ltd, to give the company its full title, had been in business for some years, and had taken over Gough's Queen of the Road at an unknown date. Their garage was at Stoke View Road, Fishponds, and this company eventually (in the 1960s) got into the extended tours market. Gough's were an old established company, running a fleet of AECs until after the war. BCS had operated coaches since at least the mid-1920s, mainly vehicles of Dennis and Thornycroft manufacture. They immediately updated the fleet with a number of Thornycrofts. These were heavy-looking beasts built in Basingstoke, purchased by Bristol Co-op and continuing that company's association with the make, numbers of which they had operated not only in their pre-war coaching fleet but among their commercial fleet for many years previously. The six later 'Thornies' were bodied by Longwell Green and returned to the body shop some years later for conversion to full front, thereby giving a much more modern appearance.

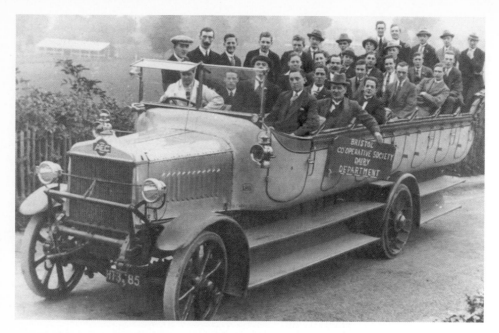

Gough's HT 3785 was a 1921 AEC.

Gough's AE 9879 was a Daimler.

Right and middle: Bristol Co-op had this 1927 Dennis, HU 8162, and in 1928 took delivery of these three Thornycrofts, nos. HW 1623-4 and 5.

By 1948 BCS had taken over Queen of the Road, Fishponds, and were operating this 1936 AEC Regal GJ8390.

1951 Sentinel/Beadle 37-
seater PAE 596.

Before ...

After ... LAE 296 &
293 Bristol Co-op 1947
Thornycroft before
and after the later
conversions to full front

WHY 825 or 826.
The two were
delivered new in
1957.

SHT 468 was a BCS
Sentinel with Plaxton
C41C body.

I remember being taken to sports afternoons every Wednesday in the Thornycrofts. These were hard-worked vehicles for several years, used consistently on contract, private hire and advertised tours duties, but were later replaced by AEC and Maudsley/Duple 35-seaters and later again by Sentinel coaches with Beadle lightweight bodies as the fleet was modernised by the Co-op. I think that the Sentinel was a very cheap integral combination, as both the chassis and body builder were trying to break into a mass market. Bedford SBs and later, AEC Regal IIIs & IVs and Maudsleys came into the fleet to be used on the UK extended tours which they had now established. The Co-op Travel department was eventually bought out by Warner's of Tewkesbury who, in partnership with the Co-op, formed Warner-Fairfax Tours. Warner's transferred some of their heavyweight vehicles to Bristol to expand their own UK and Continental tour business.

WV 5889. One of two
ex-Wilts & Dorset vehicles
which were probably the
first vehicles operated by
Sparkes (as Sparjon) in
1953.

A later acquisition.

One of the early 41-seaters

This was the Ford of Don Wiltshire mentioned in the text and which later passed to Sparkes's.

Sparkes' Coaches were situated down the hill in Warmley but had no excursion and tours licenses, to my knowledge, until they took over those of Febry's Sodbury Queen of Chipping Sodbury. Started in the early 1950s as Sparkes & Jones (t/a Sparjon Coaches) they operated from a yard in Halls Road, Kingswood. They took over an outfit called Primrose Coaches which had a base in Memorial Road, Hanham, early in their existence.

They ran several workers contracts to Filton aero-works, a few school contracts, and always seemed to be busy with Sunday fishing trips, which paid little or no return to a company anyway. I am informed that they also had contracts with rail spotters' groups, with overnight visits to all parts of the UK visiting railway engine sheds in the middle of the night. They had contracts with various hospitals for the transport of staff and, in common with just about every other operator, at one time held the prison contracts. In about 1970, Sparkes took over the licences and three seven-year-old AEC Regals IVs with Plaxton bodies of Febry's Sodbury Queen Coaches, but faded from the scene with financial difficulties shortly after. Febry's operated from Yate and Chipping Sodbury, and their coaches, in previous years, were the most luxurious around. Sold due to the family members' retirements, the fleet had been formed when their transport interests were nationalised in 1947.

A company called Streamways of Penarth had set up a small operation with (I think) three or four vehicles on the A38 at Almondsbury. Streamways held the licences for the transport of the National Servicemen based at Yatesbury and Compton Bishop etc. to weekend leave destinations and this must have been the incentive for the purchase. The services and operations were expanded and, following on from the foundations of the transport fleet, Febry's purchased heavyweight vehicles, with Fodens, AECs and Leyland Royal Tigers, bodied mainly by Plaxton's, dominating the fleet. At one time they operated as many as thirty coaches, but in latter days (by 1964) this came down to a maximum of three. In the 1950s and early '60s, they operated numerous contracts all over the country from the camps at Yatesbury etc., which provided so much weekend work that other operators were drafted in to help out. I was told by Feltham's drivers, who used to run on hire to Febry's, that they used to go to Yatesbury camp immediately after finishing the workers contracts on a Friday afternoon to pick up for just about anywhere in the UK.

The favourite destinations would be to Lancashire or London, as they would be able to contact the local operators and work for them on Saturday and Sunday doing (from Lancashire) trips to Blackpool in the summer or fishing trips on the Sunday. From London, they would work to Southend or Clacton. Either trip would give them several hours on the back seat to catch up with their sleep. They would then pick up the troops for the returns to Wiltshire area, for example, on the Sunday afternoon/evening. Newcastle upon Tyne and Glasgow were among the destinations, and I am sure that Febry's own Fodens and AECs were well used on these trips. To supplement the work, Febry's had a contract with Newman's of Yate to operate workers transport from Bristol, Filton, and Wotton-Under-Edge etc., which involved about ten coaches a day. Wessex had two coaches a day, night and morning, on permanent hire to Febry's for this work to pick up some of the Bristol workers. Ted Bleaken of Hawkesbury Upton used to operate the Wotton pick-ups, I remember. The last three vehicles operated by Febry's were 36-feet AEC/Plaxton Panoramas, with hideous leopard skin upholstery which were delivered in 1965. I do remember that at least two of the three passed to Sparkes, and that one was broken up on a farm at Kendleshire in the '70s. Their coaches were painted blue and cream, with the words 'Radio Luxury Coaches' along the roofline on each side, a style inherited from their predecessor.

Ron Pearce with Orient Coaches owned two vehicles and had very limited tours and excursions licences. Ron operated a Leyland Comet/Duple coach, together with a very old, seldom used, Leyland Cub. This business was inherited from his father.

With one vehicle only was another chap called Ray Jones. I recall that he purchased a new Thames vehicle with a Plaxton 41-seat body, and operated from his private address at the Kingsway in Kingswood, but as far as I know only ever operated a contract for BAC workers and did some private work.

DD 670 was a 1921 Reo, owned by Mr Pearce Snr.

MHT 678 was Ron Pearce's immaculate Comet

1947 Commer Commando/Plaxton

1949 Commer Avenger/Plaxton. Both were early Febry's vehicles and each came from Streamways, as can be seen from the plume of feathers displayed on the side.

One of Febry's Leyland Royal Tigers with Plaxton bodywork.

There was plenty of scope for Private Hire work in the Kingswood and South Gloucestershire area. The district abounded with very many chapels, each having their own outings etc., and a considerable amount of this work came our way. Besides the chapels, there were numerous pubs that ran several outings a year, notably to Bath and Newbury Races and Ascot being an attraction in the summer months, and these provided valuable winter work. The men would book for the races with the boot full of beer and the women would take the kids to the seaside in the summer.

One thing that must be remembered of course is that there was a glamorous side and an un-glamorous side to all of this. The glamorous side was that of being out on the road with a load of happy passengers, on holiday in the height of summer, but the other side was when the coaches had to leave the depots early on cold winter mornings to cover the workers and the later schools journeys. During the winter of 1963 the roads were covered in snow for a period of nearly SIX weeks – and we did not miss a journey. I remember that the first morning we were caught by surprise. It had snowed very heavily all night, causing severe disruption the following morning. I lived about ten minutes from the garage, and Raymond had to come to my house and get me up as drivers were late arriving or not arriving at all. I think that they all eventually made it with the exception of Stan. Peacock who normally travelled across Bristol on a motor cycle.

I covered his duty that morning and made sure that I was available and in the garage early for the next few days at least. Moravian Road was blocked at the top end by snowdrifts; one or two drivers had attempted to go that way but became stuck and could not turn around. The drivers came back to the garage and picked up other vehicles and went out the other way that morning. We removed the abandoned coaches when we got back. Then there were the previously mentioned winter private hires. Particularly during the long cold winters of the '50s and '60s, it was no fun for the driver returning in the early hours of a freezing cold Sunday morning with a drunken rugby team – knowing that when you get back to the garage you will have to thoroughly wash and disinfect the interior of the coach to clear up the remnants of the passengers' drunken night out.

In this section, I have highlighted only the operators that I encountered in the Kingswood, Staple Hill and Fishponds areas. To mention and illustrate the whole Bristol area would fill a volume and this has been achieved by an author called Colin Martin. Most of the operators mentioned worked together, if one had a vehicle shortage or breakdown they knew that one of the others would loan them a replacement – as we were the largest operator and had the most vehicles the buck usually stopped with Wessex. Most of the operators mentioned worked together, if one had a vehicle shortage or breakdown they knew that one of the others would loan them a replacement – as we were the largest operator and had the most vehicles the buck usually stopped with Wessex. Wessex may have been in competition with these operators but I think that it was more a case of friendly rivalry – everyone always helped the other at the end of the day.

CHAPTER 14

The Afterlife

Wessex Motorways Chard fleet was run down and all vehicles registered to them had been transferred back to the main fleet by the end of 1973. Raymond resigned his directorship in 1973 and began a second career lasting twenty-five years with the MOD.

On 1 August 1974 the company's express and excursion and tours licenses together with forty-two of the newest vehicles were acquired by National Travel (South West) Ltd on behalf of the National Bus Co. A dormant NBC company, Bath Tramways Motor Company Ltd was used for the transaction and was immediately renamed Wessex National Ltd to acquire the assets of Wessex Coaches (Bristol) Ltd These assets passed to NBC. The deal was completed on 21 October 1974.

Wessex Coaches Ltd retained its name, private hire facilities and certain contracts together with thirty-eight vehicles including four double-deckers but by the end of 1974 the fleet was run down to twenty-three vehicles, some of which were kept at Clifton Road – others were out-based on site. The Chard based operation at this time continued to operate in some form as did the power station contract at Heysham. In early 1975 Western National applied for and obtained the excursions and tours licenses based on Chard, Axminster, Crewkerne and Bridport. The depot then closed and was sold. The site is now a housing estate. In July 1975 the lease on the Clifton Road garage expired and this depot was closed and sold. A block of luxury flats now occupies the site. By June 1976 the remaining road service licenses were disposed of and outstanding contracts completed. The Moravian Road depot was used to house vehicles of both fleets for some time and some Wessex National vehicles had also been parked at Clifton Road until May 1975. Both fleets were seen to be working the same services for several months after the takeover. The Moravian Road depot was used by National for about five years as I recall before their vehicles were transferred back to Lawrence Hill. For time afterward, Moravian Road was used as a base for the first generation Ford Transit minibuses before the property was finally disposed of.

The Wessex Motorways company was wound up in June 1975 and the Wessex Coaches Ltd company had its share capital substantially reduced at the same time until being finally wound up in 1976. From the proceeds of the sale to National, the disposal of the surplus vehicles and the sale of the very lucrative properties, audited accounts show that there was a handsome return to the shareholders.

One can only surmise that, although the Moravian Road premises were long established as a coach-operating base the location had never previously been a 24-hour operation and for the purposes of Wessex National was way out of town. Most local people had lived there a long time and were probably not too happy with the noise that the operation would surely now create, around the clock. The yard was in the middle of a residential area. Although the space and ready-made engineering facilities would, I am sure, have been very useful to National maybe the location was not; Kingswood is 5/6 miles out of town to the Bus Station. From my experience, I could have told them of the frustrations to get a bus onto the stand at the Bristol Bus Station from Kingswood within ten minutes; it would take possibly 30/40 minutes on a busy Saturday. It sometimes did happen to us but we could always get a vehicle down from Clifton, if one was available, within the twenty minute deadline set by (then) Bristol Omnibus. Having said that, Kingswood was far more convenient if you had to get a vehicle to Bath Bus Station within the same time constriction although this probably would not have had the same advantage to Wessex National as they would now have had the facility to base vehicles at Bath (Kensington) depot.

None of the transferred vehicles lasted very long with NT as the Bedford could not really be considered a motorway vehicle among the heavyweights that were available by this time. Having said that all found new homes quite easily having been sold through dealers. It appears that most went to Ireland. The sad thing is that none of these vehicles has gone into preservation in Wessex colours. I did hear that one of the Fireflys, 944 WAE, was in a barn in the Chippenham area but that was some years ago, maybe it will resurface some day but it is certainly not listed anywhere. 946 WAE appears to survive in a very much altered form but do not be misled, the only part of this vehicle that lives on from a Wessex vehicle is most probably the registration number. It has been discovered that the chassis of this particular vehicle is that of a Bedford VAM 14, the registration number was originally LXE 556E and supplied new to Seamarks of Luton before passing to a Cornish operator from whom Mr Farrar obtained it and converted it to its current form. The chassis of such a vehicle must have been seriously 'cut and shut' from both front and rear to obtain the chassis length required by its present form.

Registered 946 WAE, but not bearing much resemblance to the original, this bus is shown working in Chester.

Two other very similar vehicles were built, each spending considerable time in the South West, 946 was the second and now appears to be the only survivor operating tours in the city of Chester.

I also understand that LAE 892L was languishing in a barn in Southern Ireland about three years ago in 2005 and was to have been preserved in its Irish owner's colours although advertised for sale, for preservation only, at £400 and later, for free. I was told that it is mechanically sound but the body is well rotted. This vehicle, from the last batch of vehicles delivered to Wessex each with Dominant bodies were among the very first of the type to be built and, as already mentioned in the tours chapter, this was the Bristol City FC coach in 1973/75 with capacity reduced to thirty-two seats. The last time that I spoke to the present owner he told me that it was then so far gone in the framework that it was literally falling to pieces stood still.

The coach was said to be sound mechanically and still retained its Bedford 466 engine although many similar were re-engined with the more powerful 500 series. At the time of writing, it was being offered free to any person or group willing to take on a preservation project. Failing this it was to be broken for spares. It's most likely gone by now. A sad end for what was once the 'cream of the fleet'.

Some people will ask why was Wessex so loyal to Bedford and Duple. The only reason that I can give for the Duple connection is that Mr Sydenham, Chairman of Duple, was also Chairman of Wessex. Maybe the business reasons for that move are obvious, Duple were protecting their own interests and ensuring continuation of supplies to a substantial customer. Why Bedford? I can only imagine that this was because of their connection with Duple, and probably Ernie Andrews and Bill Jones' relationship with both companies. Bedford vehicles were cheap and

This is a really sad picture of a YZY233 languishing in a shed in Ireland. Originally registered LAE 892L (number plate on dashboard) and pictured elsewhere. Wessex colours.

From *Buses* Magazine.

KHU 28 (ex-Maple leaf) in use as a mobile shop after it ended its passenger-carrying life. It was sold by Wessex in late 1957 and appears to have ended its passenger carrying career in March 1964.

This page and overleaf: KHU 28 survives, in a very sorry state, having been rescued from a Herefordshire hillside. One can see the size of the task in the above pictures. The remains are now in the capable hands of a very dedicated preservationist, Mr William Staniforth, but he has assured me that it will be a mammoth task to get this vehicle back together. This could be a very interesting preservation project if it ever does come to fruition, because this Bedford OB started life as a new vehicle with Maple Leaf Garages (C.W. Jordan) Ltd, and was transferred upon the formation of Wessex.

KHU 28

cheerful. Bedford was a first-class product for the price. Prior to and when they had sorted their engine problems in 1959 they had the basis of a first class touring coach and both Duple and Plaxton had for years built bodies that were suitable for that work and use in the conditions that prevailed up to the late '60s. They could keep up with the rest but when along came the motorway age, and the growing demand for continental travel, things became somewhat different. This was the beginning of the 'heavyweight' era and the more extensive use of the more powerful AEC and Leyland under floor-engined options was a massive step forward in modern design. I had this hit home to me one morning in 1966 when something happened to give an insight of what a modern vehicle, other

My PSV Driver's badge together with tow Wessex cap badges

Coach firm takeover ends family link

by DAVID HARRISON

Wessex Coaches, one of Bristol's best known coach firms, have sold their Bristol operations to National Bus Company subsidiary, National Travel

Wessex will cease independent operations on August 1 – exactly 27 years to the day that the company were formed.

But the name will live on in a new company, Wessex National Ltd., which will eventually concentrate operations on Wessex's Moravian Road, Kingswood, depot.

The takeover means the end of the link with the Jones family, who helped start Wessex in 1947, and the climax of 50 years in the coach business for director and secretary Mr. S. G. Bellamy

Wessex were formed by Mr. G. J. Jones of Morning Star Motors of Clifton Grey coaches. They bought Maple Leaf coaches and combined the three companies into Wessex.

SEVERING

Mr. Jones and Mr. Andrews are now dead but Mr. Jones's two sons, Mr. G. T. Jones and Mr. R. L. Jones, are still directors and members of the Andrews family are Wessex shareholders.

The Jones family will be severing their links with the Bristol side of the business although they will still be involved in he Chard and Heysham (Lancs) side of the company.

Mr. Bellamy will be retiring after 50 years in the coach business – and all in the same office.

He was working for Clifton Grey in their Whiteladies Road office and stayed there when Wessex was formed.

OFFERING

"It's been a seven day a week business and I've had hardly enough of it," he said today. "I shall be stayed on for a while to get matters finally sorted out and then I shall retire."

National Travel said today that they were offering jobs to all the permanents staff of Wessex an all existing bookings and commitments will be unaffected by the takeover.

The Western Area Traffic Commissioners are being asked to approve the transfer of Wessex's contracts, services and holiday tours licence to the new company.

Wessex will continue its interest in Chard and Heysham and as booking agents in Bristol.

Facsimile of article in the *Bristol Evening Post*, 1 August 1974.

than a Bedford/Duple, was really like. Smith's of Wigan (later to be a constituent company of Shearing's), had a party of American tourists staying at the Royal Hotel in Bristol. The driver had parked his coach overnight in Anchor Road; even in those days Bristol did not have a proper coach park and nothing has changed since. Someone stole it! The driver borrowed a 45-seater from Wessex at Clifton and went on his way. The vehicle was discovered a couple of hours later in Clifton and I was detailed to catch him up and bring our coach back to Bristol. This I duly did, he had got as far as Amesbury. Well, I had never perceived anything like the almost new AEC with, I think, a Plaxton body and I know that I would have enjoyed driving that around the country sat on a 'soapbox' on the chassis. What a machine! Across Salisbury Plain I think that I got the speed up to about 55mph, in comparative silence to what I was then used to, and duly got to Amesbury. The driver asked what I thought of his new steed, did I think that it went well and I told him that I was very impressed and that I had got it up to 55. He said, 'Oh, that's crawling, I have had 75 out of it'. I was left to bring an almost new VAM5 back home – there really was no comparison. Then of course came the foreign 'invasion'. Had Wessex continued in the form that I knew up to 1974 they would most certainly have had to change their buying policies even before the later demise of both the body and chassis manufacturers. Not only Wessex but very many other operators found themselves in the same predicament and this would have fed back to the likes of Bedford and Duple who, history now tells us, did not have the money or resources to fight the battle.

Why did Wessex sell? The truth is, I do not really know. Records show that the company was asset rich with no outstanding financial commitments. All vehicles were fully paid for and they were sat on a very impressive property portfolio. Each of the participating Andrews family had long since departed although the family still held shares, only the two sons of the original Jones family remained and their sons were not at all keen on entering the business. Mr Bellamy was past retirement age. Key members of staff were also ageing, Frank Davis had died in 1972 and Harry Lewis was past retirement age at the time of the sale, senior drivers and long service ancillary staff were of similar age. I know for a fact that attempts had been made to recruit younger key staff but this did not meet with much success, as in my personal case, what younger people would put up with the hours involved and impingement on private lives for not too great a wage. Added to this the excursions and tours business was ever more declining – car ownership was now the norm and people were independent. Package holidays had replaced the trips to the seaside and people were looking further and further afield to spend their leisure time. Replacement and vehicle operating costs were escalating, the days of the cheap Bedford was over and the cost of changing the fleet to heavyweights overnight would have meant a phenomenal cash outlay thus involving high interest charges in a shrinking market place.

Ten years hence and the market had gone full circle with companies geared up and catering for changed needs but those ten years, as far as Wessex was concerned, could have been the gateway to bankruptcy, so there was little choice – the offer came along and it was taken. At least that is how I have read it. Even in my days ten years previous in the 1960s it was always rumoured that, Bristol Omnibus (as it then was) would eventually take the company over – and eventually it did. But take a look at the current market place. In my day, as I have already said, at least 60% of the fleet was de-licensed and laid up – winter was considered to be the time to catch up on the maintenance with little pressure but from the 1980s onwards and becoming more and more busy as time progresses things have changed. We finished in early October, apart from the remainder of the Blackpool Illuminations tours, to the following Easter except of course for the contracts, private hire and odd trips to the races or maybe the Ideal Home Exhibition but nowadays most fleets are kept busy with 5-day midweek and 2/3 -day weekend trips, mainly taken by older people right up to Christmas when the Turkey and Tinsel and then Christmas markets are advertised. Things go quiet in January and then from mid-February it starts all over again. Rates are keener I do agree and operators will tell you that there is no money in it, OK, so they have to take a lot of money to justify the current cost of a luxury Volvo or Daf, now in excess of £200K in some cases but that is the vehicle that brings in the money.

Wessex Coaches Ltd and Wessex Coaches (Bristol) Ltd were each formally wound up in August 1976 by which time the properties had been disposed of, vehicles sold and Taylor Woodrow contracts at Heysham completed. Wessex National was still advertising a very much-reduced programme of day tours in 1982 but with a much-diminished fleet of heavyweight vehicles that were more able to stand the rigours of sustained motorway travel. Wessex National did, eventually decide to discontinue advertised tours whilst that company still ran the fleet. That fleet was heavily subsidised not only by the guaranteed 'National Express' work but also by government money until the time came for the return of private ownership.

THE END

JHY 501P (not an ex-Wessex vehicle) stands in the yard at Moravian Road c. 1975. The 'front garage' has been demolished to make room for a vehicle wash. The 'back garage' can be seen on the left. With weather such as this 501 must have been preparing for a trip to Bath Races.

Three ex-Wessex VAM 70s in National white.

MHU 926F in National white.